Walking with Ghosts on

Ward's Pond

Between the Lines
PUBLISHING

Between the Lines Publishing

Published by Between the Lines Publishing (USA)
as Liminal Books (imprint)
410 Caribou Trail, Lutsen, Minnesota 55612, USA

www.btwnthelines.com

Cover artist: Suzanne Johnson

Walking with Ghosts on Ward's Pond
Paperback: 978-1-950502-00-4

This is a work of fiction. All characters, organizations, and events portrayed are either a product of the author's imagination or are used fictitiously.

To Grace, her unborn child…and Chester…I hope you found your way home.

Rest in peace.

"It's never too late to become who you were meant to be."

- George Eliot

Prologue

THE WATER SWALLOWED HER WHOLE, the weight of her heavy skirts, corset, and unborn child dragging her down into the green, murky depths. She kicked in desperation, rising to the surface once more as a figure loomed over her, standing in the boat, his hand reaching for hers. Her fingers latched on for an instant, only to lose their grasp. The lake pulled at her once more, and this time the water won. *Chester!*

Katherine's scream bounced off the walls as she sat upright in bed, the name of a man she did not know ringing in her head. The face of a woman she'd never seen before flashed before her, and another scream tore through her as helpless tears began to fall.

A WOMAN'S SCREAM RIPPED CHARLIE from sleep as dramatically as if he'd been doused in ice water. Heart hammering in his chest, he sprang from his bed and raced to the door as another scream pierced straight through him, coming from the room across the hall. He didn't know the occupant—the only other guest currently in the bed and breakfast at Ward's Pond—but the compulsion to help…to *do* something was too great to be ignored.

"Miss? Miss, are you all right? Can I help you?" He pressed his ear to the wall, hearing nothing more than a muffled sobbing. "I only want to help you and make sure that you're all right. I'm coming in."

When no response came, Charlie gathered up his courage and grabbed hold of the knob, taking a quick glance at his clothes. Thankfully, he wore modest pajama bottoms and a T-shirt, nothing that would scandalize anyone. After one hard swallow, he gave the door a try, surprised to find it unlocked. He glanced across the room to see a woman sitting up in bed. The moon cast her in white, making her look ghostly. Her long, dark hair was a wild tangle, the tracks of her tears glistening in the light streaming through the window. She was trembling.

Unwilling to seem too familiar or forward, Charlie pulled up a chair—rather than sitting on the end of the bed. He leaned toward her and propped his elbows on his knees, striving to offer her a calm, reassuring presence when all the while his insides were churning from that terrible screaming.

"Is everything all right? What happened?"

The stranger took a shaky breath and drew the covers up to her chest, her knuckles bulging with the strength of her grip. "I…it was just a nightmare. Foolish, really. I can't even remember it now…I can only recall waking up feeling absolutely terrified."

He nodded and then gave her a smile. "I know what that's like. My name is Charlie Baxter and I'm right across the hall. If you need anything—anything at all—don't hesitate to give a knock. I sleep light."

He stood as she extended her hand—which he accepted, giving it a squeeze. His skin practically sizzled at her touch, but he held on. "Thank you, Mr. Baxter. I'm sorry I woke you."

"Nonsense. Like I said, I sleep light! I would've been up sooner or later anyway, and please, call me Charlie. My *father* is Mr. Baxter. I'll see you at breakfast in the morning. Our hostess, Eva, is an amazing cook." Charlie crossed the room, taking pause at the door to look over his shoulder. "By the way, what's your name?"

She smiled, and it was like the sun coming out after a storm. "Katherine. Katherine Grace Brown."

The name, particularly the middle and last, gave him a start, but he covered it well. "Well, Miss Katherine Grace Brown, may the rest of your night hold nothing but sweet dreams."

As he crossed the hall, the turning of the lock broke the silence. Charlie didn't think she was locking *him* out. Katherine was locking herself—and her mysterious nightmares—in.

Unable to sleep, since his mind was already unsettled from his research, Charlie opened the window and took a deep gulp of the refreshing night air. Late May in upstate New York heralded warmer days and the approach of summer, but the nights were still chilly. He left the window open, flicked on his desk lamp, and riffled through his stacks of papers, his hand landing on the picture of Grace Brown. He stared at the image that was already imprinted on his brain. *She looks nothing like that girl across the hall. Her name is just a coincidence.*

He started taking notes, but still a voice nagged at him at the back of his mind. *Is there really any such thing as a coincidence?*

1

CHARLIE SCRAPED A HAND ACROSS HIS FACE and sipped his coffee, trying to shake his fatigue. Between his work and the mysterious guest across the hall, he'd only caught a few hours of sleep. After another sip of coffee, he nodded his thanks to his hostess as she dropped off his breakfast at the dining room table. It felt almost sinful to have someone serve him this way. He was a confirmed bachelor, accustomed to fending for himself. *You're paying for every cent of this; don't forget that.* The reminder made it easier to enjoy the food laid before him. An omelette chock-full of vegetables. Fresh fruit. Wheat toast. Just what the doctor ordered to help him get some pep in his step.

He started to tuck away his breakfast, staring out into a sumptuous sitting room with antique wooden furniture polished to a high gleam. An Oriental rug worth a small fortune dressed the floor. It was almost a shame to walk on it; it made Charlie want to kick off his shoes every time he crossed the room like he used to do at his grandparents' place in Rhinebeck. Vintage lamps with milky globes sat atop tables throughout the house while chandeliers dangled overhead. At one point in time, this place had been ritzy, but it was more like an archaic museum now.

As he dabbed at his mouth with a linen napkin, Charlie's gaze traveled to the porch—or *veranda,* as his mother would say. It was all too easy to imagine he was the well-to-do owner of the home in Dolgeville, a village that once held a great deal of wealth over a century ago when the Daniel Green factory created an economic hub for the community.

Charlie shied away from that image, because he didn't want to be associated with the owner of *this* particular home and the way the man had earned his keep to do so well. A portrait of Judge George Ward was at his back, making him feel like eyes were searing into him uncomfortably. He concentrated on a warm breeze drifting in through the window, setting the tall grasses and flowers to swaying.

His eyes drooped closed. It was so hard to keep them open. *Grace.* A voice whispered hoarsely in his ear. Charlie snapped back to attention and glanced over his shoulder. A dark-haired man whose brooding eyes burned with emotion stood at the doorway, his hand extended. Charlie felt the air shift with a woman's passing, her flowing skirt brushing against him. She was fair skinned with dark hair piled on top of her head. He caught the curve of her cheek and the glisten of eyes—a soft brown, as gentle as a doe's. A jolt in his chair made his body jerk, and Charlie forced himself to look outside. *There's no one there! You have got to stop staying up all night doing research. Get some sleep.*

FOR AN INSTANT, KATHERINE THOUGHT SHE WAS ROCKING. She could hear the quiet lapping of the water slapping against the side of the boat and feel the weight of her heavy skirts pulling her down again. A scream clawed its way out of her throat and she shot up, only to open her eyes and sag back against the pillows in relief. She was in bed. At the bed and breakfast on Ward's Pond, where the darkness slowly gave way to light with the coming of the dawn.

It was just a dream, silly. Only another dream. A flood of nightmares had been troubling her regularly since her marriage fell apart. She couldn't make heads or tails out of most of them. With that realization, the sadness came rolling in, pressing her flat against the mattress as if a stone was resting on her chest. One hand trailed to her hollow stomach. *Alone. You are completely alone.* The sorrow weighed so heavily on her that Katherine wasn't sure she could ever move again.

Probably the reason for those terrible dreams. A metaphor for your loneliness. She let loose a sigh and considered going back to sleep, but there was an undercurrent of dread running beneath the surface of her mind that made her reluctant to return to the terrifying landscape of her dreams. An image of Charlie, her midnight rescuer, sprang into her mind. His face was cast in the silver glow of the moon, those soulful eyes staring at her. And only her.

Hope tinged with trepidation had her springing out of bed and heading straight for the shower to start primping. After all, Cinderella dressed up for the ball, and she'd never even seen *her* prince. Katherine caught a glimpse of hers under the moonlight in the wee hours of the morning. Now she was hungry to see him in the glory of sunlight. *Guess who's coming to breakfast?*

THE WOMAN FROM ACROSS THE HALL HESITATED FOR A HEARTBEAT in the entranceway of the dining room, her eyes searching. The tumble of her deep brown curls was like a river running down her back. They cascaded over a flowing dress in pale green that brought out the color of her eyes, a hint of summer hiding in their grassy depths. Her gaze landed on Charlie, and a slow smile made her mouth pull up at the corners. He found himself frozen and tongue-tied, not the combination one desired when it came to making good impressions.

She extended her hand to him. "Charlie…nice to meet you in the daylight. It's good to see a familiar face this morning. I was afraid I might be the only guest here."

He gained his feet quickly and accepted her handshake. The sensation was electric, a current of attraction running straight to his head. Seeing the flush of her skin, Charlie figured she felt something, too. To cover his agitation, he pulled out a chair with a slight bow. "The pleasure is mine. I take it you slept well the rest of the night?"

Her eyes were shadowed for an instant, but her smile banished the darkness. "Like a baby." Charlie couldn't hide a grin. This woman was most definitely *not* a baby.

Eva returned with a silver serving tray. The woman had impeccable timing. Charlie wondered if she hovered with her ear pressed to the wall, waiting for someone to sit down at the table. "Good morning, Miss Katherine. Can I interest you in coffee or tea this morning?"

"Tea would be lovely, Eva. Thank you."

Eva set the tray down on the sideboard and poured a strong brew from a china teapot. She proceeded to set the steaming cup in front of her guest, as well as cream and sugar, tastefully displayed in silver servers. "More coffee, sir?" she inquired cheerfully as Charlie simply held out his cup. "You're sure you don't want any cream or sugar, sir?"

Charlie couldn't help but chuckle. "We've been through this, Eva. I'm already sweet enough! Besides, I need my coffee strong to disentangle my mind from mountains of research at night."

"Learn anything new yet, sir?" She paused beside him, staring intently. The woman had a vested interest in the outcome of his story.

Charlie waved her off. "Not yet, Eva. And *please*, call me Charlie. You make me feel too damned old calling me *sir* all the time or as if I'm putting on airs."

Eva laughed, a rich sound that dispelled any of the lingering darkness caused by his restless night. She squeezed his shoulder, pushing her short, dark curls out of dark eyes that snapped. The woman

8

reminded Charlie of a gypsy. He suspected that she could read his mind or foretell his future. "What will you have for breakfast, Miss Katherine?"

"How about toast and yogurt? Thank you." As the hostess slipped out of the room, Katherine shook her head. "I don't feel like I should be telling Eva what I want. I'm perfectly capable of going in the kitchen and preparing my own breakfast."

"I know but remember that this is part of the experience and lends the setting a certain kind of charm." Charlie pushed his empty plate away and then patted his stomach. "Not to mention, Eva is one fine cook."

The woman in question returned a few minutes later, setting a plate in front of Katherine. It was impressive, showcasing a deep dish of vanilla yogurt topped with an artfully arranged blend of fresh fruits, as a lightly browned toast sat beside it on a dainty plate made of china. Attentive as always, Eva filled Charlie's cup once again, even when he tried to stop her. She only smiled fondly at him, asking brightly, "Anything else I can get for you two?"

Katherine shook her head. "No; this is perfect." As she took a bite, a book on the table snagged her attention. "Eva, before you go, what's the story behind that *Murder in the Adirondacks* book lying there?" She paled upon posing the question. Was she sensitive to the subject matter, perhaps?

Eva's eyes lit up and she pulled a chair over, grabbing a cup of coffee off the tray. Upon sitting down, she settled in to dish gossip as skillfully as she'd served delicacies from her kitchen. "Oh, quite the scandal that was, and Judge Ward, the former owner of *this* very house," she said and motioned to the portrait on the wall, "...played a major role in what was the trial of the century at the time. Back in 1906, a skirt factory owner's nephew got a poor factory worker pregnant. He took her off on a rowboat on Big Moose Lake...and the girl didn't make it back."

Katherine's eyes went wide as she stared at the cover of the book depicting a man and woman struggling in a boat. "Can I read it sometime?"

Eva finished her coffee with a sigh, jumping to her feet again. "Goodness, yes! Anytime you wish. There are copies of that book everywhere in this old house. Judge Ward was the district attorney and the prosecutor at the time, and he made sure they found that filthy murderer guilty. We figure guests will want to read about it once they hear of the judge's connection to the case. There's a copy right out there in the parlor, if you care to borrow it."

Eva caught Charlie's disapproving stare and began to blush. "Sorry, Charlie. I know you have strong views about the case and the flip side of the coin. I'm sure you're tired of rehashing it." With that, she returned to the kitchen to attend to the rest of her hostess duties.

Tired. She's got that right. Gulping down his coffee to wake up, Charlie focused on the girl beside him. Katherine made it hard to concentrate, with her lilac-scented perfume drifting his way. His head became filled with images that were quite refreshing after being mired in the past and his research for too long.

He waited until she was done eating and then asked quietly, "Care to go outside and walk the grounds…you know, to get some fresh air?"

Katherine nodded and left the table, stepping into the parlor. The wind passed through the open screen door, sending another scent his way—of something sweet and unfamiliar. Honeysuckle, perhaps? Softly, as if from far away, he could hear someone singing, "Won't you come home, Bill Bailey?" A voice filled with longing whispered in his ear. *Grace.*

Shut up, Chester! Charlie stood up and trailed after his fellow guest at the inn. He didn't dare look over his shoulder for fear that he'd see the dark-haired man of his research—the same man who was found guilty of killing Grace Brown and was then sentenced to death in *Murder in the Adirondacks*—and visualize nightmares standing behind him.

2

KATHERINE PUSHED THE SCREEN DOOR OPEN, relishing the way it creaked, just like the farmhouse where she grew up. The air was mild and kissed her skin, trailing through her hair, enveloping her in the scent of an explosion of flowers surrounding the stately old home dressed in a pale butter yellow. She closed her eyes and tried to pick out a particular type of flower, pulling honeysuckle out of the mix. It crept up a stone wall and latticework, one of nature's eye-catching tapestries at its best.

Steps sounded behind her and Charlie joined her, taking in the view of the East Canada Creek as it rushed by on the other side of the road, a flock of geese flying overhead. She followed their path and watched them touch down on the large pond that extended in the distance only a few feet from the grand porch. "My goodness! That pond is more like an ocean. Let's see it up close."

"All right. After you," Charlie agreed with a bow. Katherine took the steps slowly but caught her shoe and nearly stumbled when a strong hand took her elbow, proving it was attached to an even stronger arm. "Careful now," he warned her with a wink, continuing to hold on like gentlemen callers from days of old.

With his white button-down shirt sleeves rolled to the elbows, dark dress pants, and a brown medley of wavy hair falling over his eyes, Charlie looked the part. Katherine had to stifle a giggle, half expecting her father to appear on a porch rocker with a shotgun, standing guard.

They walked along the front lawn for several feet, following the creek's wild progress, which was filled to nearly overflowing after heavy rains and the meltdown of winter's snow coming down off the mountains. Charlie picked up a rock and flung it across the street. They could hear a satisfying *plunk*.

"How do you like the quaint little village of Dolgeville? It was really something in its heyday, thanks to the Daniel Green shoe and slipper factory. This used to be *the* place to be, but now it's just a small collection of businesses and beautiful old homes." He gestured off to the left. "You should've seen the Alfred Dolge mansion over on Dolge Ave. The town founder's home was over a century old and had forty-four rooms. A true gem and piece of history, but it burned down not too long ago. A real shame."

Katherine eyed him, her mouth turning up in a grin. "Well, aren't you just a fount of information. I didn't know I'd be getting a tour guide."

"Sorry. I'm a journalist working on my first book. I've done a lot of research about the area. If I start sounding like I'm rattling off an encyclopedia, just whack me upside my ear." Charlie ducked his head, but not before she caught a flash of blue eyes fringed by some of the darkest lashes she'd ever seen. They gave her heart a hiccup and made her catch her breath even as she lost her footing again. She needn't have worried. He had her in his sturdy grip.

"That's all right." She gave his arm a squeeze at his dubious look. "No, really. I think it's interesting."

They made their way slowly to the pond, acting as if they had all the time in the world. The water extended a long way off into the distance, one of the largest ponds Katherine had ever seen. Surrounded

12

by weeping willows that trailed their branches in the water, there was a heavy smattering of plants creeping up along its shores. Lily pads formed a carpet of green, creating an illusion one could walk across the surface. The place looked like something out of a storybook.

"It's like a fairytale. If I reach down and catch a frog, do you think he'll turn into a prince and make me a princess?" Katherine knelt by the bank and reached for a bullfrog that leapt and splashed them both, making them laugh.

"You're already too much like a princess. That frog must have been confused." Charlie offered her a hand and then led her to one of several benches that provided pleasant seating arrangements for any of the patrons staying at Ward's Pond.

Katherine sat down carefully, arranging the folds of her dress neatly while Charlie leaned back and tilted his head to the sky, closing his eyes and inhaling deeply of the fresh air. "God, that smells good."

She couldn't help but stare at the fluttering pulse at the base of his neck and the dark hairs curling before hiding beneath his shirt—the same dark hairs trailing down his bare forearms. His hair was a blend of browns, like the samples of stains in the hardware store back home when she was growing up. Cherry. Walnut. Maple. Chestnut. Light in some places kissed by the sun, darker at the nape of his neck—that delightful spot that just begged to be kissed.

Growing warm and fearing a flush would soon be creeping up her neck to her hairline, Katherine nudged his arm with her elbow, seeking a distraction. "What brings you here to Ward's Pond and the sleepy village of Dolgeville?"

"*I WANT TO BE ABLE TO SLEEP AGAIN.*" Charlie nearly bit his tongue, surprised at himself. There was something about the quiet, dark-haired girl with such soulful eyes—seemingly much older than her years—that made him open with painful honesty.

"I don't understand," she said softly as her hand found its way to his. There was a jolt at the moment of contact that made his heart skip a beat. Charlie wondered if he'd ever get used to being touched by this woman.

He tried to grin, but it slipped away. Charlie stood and walked to the edge of the pond, and Katherine followed. He reached down, scooped up a handful of rocks, and skipped them on the water. The noise startled some geese that were tucked in the tall weeds. They soon took flight, mesmerizing the couple as the majestic birds flew overhead, navigating a return trip to the creek. Katherine's hand gave an insistent squeeze. She just wasn't giving up.

"I haven't been able to sleep for the last month or so since I started working on my book. Every time I close my eyes, this *Murder in the Adirondacks* story grabs hold of my mind. It's the kind of story that gets under my skin. Poking at me. Pushing me to dig deeper. Telling me there's more to the case than what they found out back in 1905, '06…whatever it is. Right now, I feel like my brain's Swiss cheese. So tired I can't keep anything straight. Damn the journalist in me. If I think there's another side of a story that needs to be told, it won't let go of me until I tell it." Charlie ran a hand through his hair. "I just want a little peace."

Katherine smiled at him. "Me too." She darted in boldly, dropping a feather brush of a kiss on his jawline. "I hope you find it."

His cheek burned from the brush of her lips against his skin while his hand tingled. He felt a strange sense of connection with this young woman, one he couldn't deny. They took a stroll around to another side of the pond and settled on an iron bench with intricate scrollwork to watch more geese. Babies followed their mother, creating a chain on the water. Katherine's face lit up as she pressed her palm to her cheek. "Look at them. How adorable!"

Her hand was still in his, and Charlie couldn't help but feel like it had found a home there. "Enough about me. What led you here and why do *you* need to find some peace?"

It was as if shutters went down over those creek-water eyes, and then her lip turned up at the corner in a forced smile. "I've had a streak of bad luck with men. The latest ended in divorce. All I wanted to do was get away for a while, so I sold the house, put most everything in storage, and then left. I packed up, got in the car, and drove. I didn't have a plan or use a GPS, yet it was like my car decided to take me here. I don't know. It was the strangest thing. It felt like this old house was calling to me. The moment I set foot on the porch, I was welcomed home. Weird."

Charlie sat up straight, suddenly animated as his hand tightened on hers. "Me too! I mean, I did a bit of research and decided to check the place out because of Judge Ward's connection to Chester and Grace, the star players in that book Eva told you about. I could have stayed at so many other places, like Big Moose Lake where she died—or Old Forge, one of their stops along the way. Ward's Pond could've been just a stopping point, but something pulled at me to stay here..."

The woman beside him became a shade whiter, her hand cold in his. "You all right? You look like you've seen a ghost."

CHESTER. THE NAME HAD TO BE A COINCIDENCE. Katherine stared out over the pond and on the other side, she saw a woman walking along the shore. She was dressed in white, her dark hair piled up high on her head, her face unspeakably sad. The woman in my dream?!

She swallowed hard, concentrating on Charlie's voice beside her. "No, I think my coffee and my restless night have caught up with me, giving me the jitters. Maybe I'll go lie down for a while." Katherine looked across the pond again. The image was now gone. No more ghost stories for you before bed. She had picked up a book in town—Ghosts in the Adirondacks—on her way to the bed and breakfast. What had she been thinking? She'd always had an overactive imagination.

15

Being a true gentleman, Charlie stood and offered her his hand. "That's not a bad idea. I might do the same—if this story will let me." On that teasing note, they walked back to the house and parted ways.

Katherine suspected that her new acquaintance would be immersing himself in his quest for information about a truly cold case in every sense of the word. She rested for a little while, but a lingering unease and sadness followed her that wouldn't let her sleep. She walked the few blocks into town for a quiet lunch, munching on a sandwich and sipping a soda from a convenience shop, while sitting on a bench by the East Canada Creek. She hummed to herself, surprised when an old tune her grandmother had loved—"Bill Bailey, Won't You Please Come Home?"—popped into her mind. For some reason, the song soothed her, and she walked back to Ward's Pond with a lighter heart.

A chat with Eva led to her being dragged into her hostess's private sitting room to watch her favorite soap opera, which carried over to a classic movie. Yawning and begging off that she was tired, Katherine bade her a good evening and headed upstairs. Funny, it had been a day of doing nothing and it simply flew by. She suddenly wondered how Charlie was making out.

She hesitated outside his room, debating on whether to knock or let him be. The grumbling of her stomach decided the matter. The man had to eat, so she might as well see if he'd join her. Katherine tapped on the door to no response. Leaning in close, she could hear nothing. Remembering his open invitation to help her at any time, she cautiously tried the knob.

The door swung open to reveal a room much like her own, with antique furniture and an old light that looked like a kerosene lamp illuminating the room. The window was open, making the curtains dance in the breeze and giving Katherine a chill with the temperature drop that signaled the approach of nightfall.

Charlie was sound asleep at his desk, his head resting on a stack of papers, his hair shielding his eyes. His laptop was open, books were scattered everywhere, and a collection of old photographs was spread out around him. His hand rested on one. Too curious for her own good, Katherine slipped in next to him to get a closer look. At a man…and a woman.

She bent down even lower, her hair brushing his arm, and her throat began to close. There they were: Chester Gillette and Grace Brown. The precise people from her dream the night before. On the boat. Fear clutched at her heart and made her start to sway.

CHARLIE WORKED DILIGENTLY ON HIS NOTES, accumulating more data, rereading the same page over and over until the words blurred together. He dragged his hands across his face. *Need to close my eyes. Just for a minute.*

He was rocking gently from side to side on a calm lake, surrounded by a thick stand of pines. Charlie could smell the heady scent of the evergreens and hear water lapping at the side of the boat. It was a summertime night, lit up by starlight and the glow of the moon. He was filled with an overwhelming sense of sadness and frustration. It pinned him down as he stared into the black surface of the lake, as though it were a crystal ball and he searched it for answers. If he fell overboard, it would drown him. At that moment, he'd welcome such a fate.

A child? What do I do with a child? I can't marry her, can't be a father…they'll fire me at the factory! What good will I be then? I'll have nothing…yet again! The same thoughts that had been circling around in his brain for months continued to snap at his peace of mind like sharks ripping into their prey.

Charlie glanced up to see a woman perched on the seat at the other end of the boat, her dark eyes glistening in the moonlight, skin turning to silver. She pleaded with him without saying a word. "*Grace*…I just don't know what to do…I think…I think you need to go to a home for unwed mothers…just until the baby's born…and then you can pick up your life again. It will seem like nothing ever happened. You'll see."

"Without you? What will I do without you, Chester? I don't want to live without you…" She stood up suddenly, intent on closing the gap between them.

"Grace! *Grace*, sit down before you fall!" Charlie shouted and lunged for her, but everything seemed like it was in slow motion. She tripped, hitting her head on the side of the boat as she went over. He tried to catch her, but he was just too clumsy. Too slow. Too late.

Her heavy dress was too cumbersome, and it dragged her down. *Blast those dresses, petticoats, layers upon layers!* All the way to the bottom. Even as her hand reached for him, he couldn't grab it. *"GRACE!"*

Charlie woke up with a jerk, his head snapping up. *A dream! You know it was just a dream. You've got all this rigmarole working your mind overtime and it's making up your happy—well, not-so-happy—ending. There's no way you could be channeling Chester to get his side of the story. It's just what you want it to be and you know it. An accident. A likely story. He was probably a cold-blooded, heartless son of a bitch.*

Even as the thoughts battered against his overtired skull, Charlie's face stung like he'd been slapped. His mother would've washed his mouth out with soap for such language and then sent him to confession before their priest. Charlie made the sign of the cross and murmured an apology for speaking ill of the dead, his hand grazing the photographs on his desk that he'd stared at too many times. Only then did he notice Katherine standing beside his desk, her hand on her chest, looking frightened. "Katherine, what's wrong?"

"I wanted to see if you'd like to go to dinner with me. It's a lovely evening. We could walk up to town, see what we can find. I couldn't wake you when I knocked so I decided to come in. You practically gave me a heart attack when you jumped up from your chair. Maybe I should leave you alone." She inched toward the door.

"No! I know where we can go. Arthur's is a great place. Good food, plenty of local character. Just let me clean up." Charlie went to the bathroom and ran a comb through his hair. He closed his eyes for a moment, centering himself. When he opened his eyes, Chester was in the mirror, standing next to him. *What the hell do you want?*

Charlie splashed water on his face, and his ghostly visitor was gone. *You're going out of your mind. Take a break.* He popped his head back in his doorway to see Katherine standing at the window, staring out at the pond, her face filled with such longing it made him ache inside. Putting on some false cheer, Charlie crossed the room and touched her shoulder. "Are you ready?"

She smiled and set her hand in his. They walked downstairs, bidding Eva a good night as they headed for the porch. Charlie caught a glimpse of Judge Ward's portrait and felt his accusing stare drilling a hole in the back of his skull. *Don't look at me. I didn't kill her.* Resolutely turning his eyes forward, he stepped outside with Katherine. Chester and Grace would have to stay behind for a night.

3

THE CREEK BURBLED ALONGSIDE THEM, its low hum providing musical accompaniment for their walk on a moonlit night. Somehow, Katherine's hand was nestled in Charlie's once again, and it felt right. Mentally, he started to argue with himself. *Don't question it. Lots of strange things have been happening since you dug into this case. At least this is something good.*

Katherine started singing halfway there, giving him a start. "Won't you come home, Bill Bailey," she sang—of all things. She cut herself off, laughing self-consciously. "Sorry. I don't know why that song has been stuck in my head all day. My grandmother had one of those old Victrolas, you know? The kind you'd wind up with a great big arm and needle that you would then set down on a thick, old record. I used to play it all the time and dance with my dolls around the living room."

Grace's favorite song. Another coincidence? A cold sweat broke out on Charlie's face as his heart began to trip. He fought to rein it in, chuckling weakly. "Sounds like we have a lot in common. My grandparents used to play the oldies, too…on an antique radio at their house in Rhinebeck. I'd spend the summers there. I grew up in Saratoga and still have an apartment there. How about you?"

"Right now, I don't live anywhere. My husband and I used to live in Syracuse." Katherine frowned as she dug her toe into the dirt alongside the road, dislodging a rock and sending it clattering down to the river. "I grew up on my grandparents' farm in Galway with my mother." She paused while her forehead creased, hinting at her agitation. "It would appear she had the same luck with men that I do. My father took off before I was born." She looked up at him shyly. "Maybe I've finally broken the streak with you. You're a *nice* guy."

Charlie's stomach twisted into a knot. He didn't feel like such a nice guy, not since the Gillette-Brown murder case had consumed his life. "I'd wait before you make any final judgments about me. When I'm caught up in a project, I tend to get carried away, forget to pay attention to anything—or anyone—around me. You might find me buried up to my ears in dusty old books and articles."

"Well, I'll come dig you out when you need to see the light of day again." Her fingers applied pressure on his, drawing him in.

Before Charlie knew it, his mouth was sealing hers. The scent of lilacs, the perfume dusting her skin, everything blended with the coconut shampoo in her hair to surround him. The warmth of her skin against his made him forget—just for a night—about Chester and Grace or anything else that happened over one hundred years ago. And if he'd stand there long enough, he mused, he'd probably forget who he was.

They both had to come up for air. Charlie rested his forehead against hers. "I feel like I'm blinded right now. I can't see anything—except you."

Katherine's fingers trailed up his arm, threading through his hair. "Me either."

CHARLIE SAT ACROSS FROM HER AT A HIGH TABLE in the bar. There'd been room in the main dining area, but both preferred the more casual, intimate setting in the tavern section. The bed and breakfast on

Ward's Pond gave them plenty of class. Katherine raised her hard cider to Charlie. "To new beginnings."

He clinked his bottle of beer with hers. "And to leaving the past behind." They both took a sip before his breath came out in a rush. She could hear the tapping of his fingers on the scratched surface of the glossy oak, outward signs of some inner battle. Charlie leaned forward and his voice dropped down low. "Listen, Katherine. Before we go any farther, I feel like I must be completely honest with you so you can make your decisions about me with your eyes wide open, okay?"

She took a long tug on her drink and set it down. "Sure. Hit me with it. You're married and you have five kids...no! That's not it. You're gay and this whole research thing is a sham. You just want to meet secretly with your lover, the gardener."

Charlie started to laugh so hard he choked on his beer. He grabbed his napkin and covered his mouth while he sputtered. "Wrong on both counts. I am straight and single. *Painfully* single." He took a swig of liquid courage, setting his shoulders.

"The reason that I'm in this Gillette-Brown case so deep is because I'm distantly related to Chester. I grew up hearing about it in hushed whispers at family gatherings. Sometimes, there would be heated arguments. No matter what, it was like there was this dark cloud hanging over us that we could never quite shake. Occasionally, it would drift off in the distance, but it was always there. That's why my mother begged me to look into it once I became a journalist. For some peace at last. Closure."

The words ran dry as he picked up his beer, taking long swallows until the bottle

was empty. Only then did Charlie look her in the eye. "I'll understand if you don't want to have anything to do with me."

Katherine took his hand in both of hers. "Charlie, don't be ridiculous. *You* didn't do anything wrong, and besides, that happened over a hundred years ago. Why should I want to stay away from *you*?

Besides, I agree that there are always two sides to every tale. Maybe you're meant to uncover the untold story about Chester and Grace."

Charlie bowed his head, his eyes drifting closed. "Sometimes I feel like this story is a steel trap and its teeth are digging into me. They really won't let me go."

"Maybe I can help. I've got nothing else to do while I'm here. I could be your research assistant." She continued to hold on to his hand, trying to ease his burden. Charlie looked up at her and his body went loose at her touch, the tension fading.

"I just might take you up on that." Their waitress arrived at that moment, setting down two plates with the evening special, a fresh fish fry. The couple was quiet, enjoying their meal. When his plate was nearly empty, Charlie leaned back and waved his hand. "That's it. I am so done."

Katherine took one last bite and set her plate on his. "You're right. That was the best I've had in a long time. I really like this place. Over a hundred years old, eh? Too bad you can't stay upstairs in the inn anymore. I bet that was something you'd never forget in an old building like this...so rich in history. Kind of like the bed and breakfast."

Charlie fished out his wallet and peeled off a few bills, placing them on the table. Katherine protested, but he only shook his head. "My treat. I insist. You're new in town. This is your welcome dinner." He was kind but firm.

There was no sense arguing. "Thank you. I'll return the favor." Katherine accepted his hand and they began the walk back to Ward's Pond, taking their time. She could hear the sound of running water. The creek never stopped. For an instant, she was in that boat again, falling overboard.

Katherine stopped suddenly, pulling her hand from Charlie's, rubbing at her arms. "There's something...something I have to tell you, too. My ex-husband, Mike...the divorce isn't finalized. It's been long and messy. Believe me when I tell you that it's over between us, but I don't know when it'll finally be official. That's why I came here. To get away from him. This is your chance to walk away from *me*, seeing as I'm still married on paper and I come with a tractor trailer's truckload of baggage."

Charlie stepped in closer, his hands resting on her arms, warming her with his touch. His cologne—something earthy and hypnotic—calmed her fears, the same way he had in the middle of the night after her nightmare. "You can use a friend, right? So can I."

They continued the walk home, his arm around her to ward off the cool night air. He accompanied her to her door, leaning on the door jamb while she put her key in the lock. "Thanks for everything, Charlie. Make sure you get some sleep tonight."

He bent down and kissed her, a gentle brush of his lips against hers. "You do the same. Remember, I'm just across the hall if you need me."

Katherine closed the door and leaned up against it. She'd been confused in the last year, as her world had been turned upside down when the man she thought was Mr. Right turned into Mr. Wrong, but there was one thing she knew for sure. She wanted the man across the hall to be more than a friend. Stretching out on her bed, Katherine focused on just one thing. Sweet dreams of Charlie Baxter. With her eyes wide open.

CHARLIE TRIED TO TAKE HER ADVICE. He left his laptop on his desk, unopened. Pushed all the papers into their appropriate folders. Switched the light off. In the dark, he slipped out of his clothes—down to his plain white T-shirt and boxers. The fresh air drifting through his window felt good, so he left it open. He slid between blessedly cool sheets and turned on his side, holding tightly to his spare pillow. In his mind, Katherine was in his arms and she was heating up the room to the point of a meltdown.

Unable to sleep with that image in his head, he rolled over on his back and began to replay all the moments they'd spent together in his mind. Their first encounter, late at night. Breakfast. Their morning stroll to the pond. Arthur's. That unbelievable kiss. Charlie relived it, pondering how it was even possible that they barely knew each other, but they could gel so well. Focusing on Katherine, the scent of her filling his lungs, her touch soothing the raw places inside of him, he finally drifted off and dreamed—of the day he found out the blood of a murderer ran in his veins.

He was fourteen, arriving home after the mile walk from school. It was hot; Charlie was dripping with sweat and parched to the bone. He rooted around in the fridge and pulled out a jug of iced tea. Glancing from side to side out of the corner of his eyes to make sure there were no witnesses, he tipped his head back and started guzzling the cold brew down, right from the bottle. When he couldn't possibly drink another swallow, a great sigh escaped him, and his arm swiped across his mouth. He then set the tea back in the fridge, dropped his backpack in the corner, and grabbed an apple out of the bowl of fruit on the counter. Maybe the other kids in the neighborhood could be persuaded to play some backyard baseball and take a dip in the swimming hole deep in the woods.

What about your homework? *A nagging voice—his conscience, most likely—buzzed at the back of his mind. He swatted it away like an irritating fly. With only three more weeks of school left, homework would keep until later that evening. Daylight was a-wasting.*

Taking the stairs two at a time, Charlie hurried upstairs, intent on finding his baseball mitt, ball, and bat. He pulled up short at the sound of crying behind his mother's closed bedroom door. He stepped up to the thick, solid oak and rested a tentative hand on its smooth surface. His mother was a strong woman. It would take a great deal to make her dissolve in tears.

Charlie tapped softly. "Mom? Are you all right?" She mumbled a yes and cried even harder. Not satisfied with her answer, he took a deep breath and stepped into her room.

She was sitting on the bed; a pile of pictures, letters, and books was scattered around her, with some stacked on the floor, some in her lap, and others on the dresser. Papers were crumpled, some were torn, and Mom looked like she'd been sobbing for hours.

Slowly, Charlie approached the bed and tentatively rested a hand on her shoulder. "Mom, what is it? What's wrong?" His heart picked up the pace as fear set in. He was afraid that something terrible happened, that someone had died. His hand tightened its grip. "Did something happen to Dad?" His father was in the service. Charlie and his mother both lived in trepidation of the moment they'd get that call or the messenger at the door.

She shook her head, swiping at her cheeks. "No, no. Nothing like that. Everything's okay, baby."

He glanced at the papers on her bed—at a picture of a young woman with sad, dark eyes and a young man who looked strangely familiar. "What's all this? Did one of our relatives die or something?" She buried her face in her hands. Charlie sat beside her and wrapped his arm around her shoulders. "Mom, you're scaring me. What's going on?"

Somehow, she pulled herself together, telling him about their distant relative, Paul Gillette, and Paul's brother, Chester. She also told him about a pregnant young woman who had been murdered in the heart of the Adirondacks on a cold, lonely lake. A family shame and mystery ate away at his mother. That afternoon, as the dying light of day faded and he noticed streaks of gray in Jenny Baxter's hair, Charlie felt like he'd been bitten by a venomous snake as the poison of the Gillette-Brown murder seeped into his veins...and began gnawing on him.

It never stopped. *Grace.* The voice rang out in his mind, the same one he heard whether waking or sleeping, dragging him up from the depths of his dream. Charlie pressed an arm over his eyes. He *wouldn't* look. *Grace...please!*

"Please leave me alone!" Charlie lunged out of bed and flicked on the lamp. He sat down at his desk, fired up the laptop, and then picked up the file that included detailed records from the trial concerning Chester Gillette's journey that began at the Gillette Skirt Factory in 1905 and ultimately took him to Big Moose Lake, ending in the electric chair in Auburn Prison. Charlie worked through the night until daylight streamed through his window, his eyes were too tired to see anymore, and his mind was much too worn to pull up any more images of Chester. Finally, he slept.

SHE WAS RESTLESS. Katherine couldn't relax. She fiddled with the piano, picking out keys. When that wasn't enough of a distraction, she strolled around the room, examining knickknacks on the shelves, reading the descriptions beneath photos and paintings. She dropped down on the sofa and let out a big sigh until suddenly, *Murder in the Adirondacks* caught her eye. Debating for an instant, she opened it and began to read. She was sucked in quickly, remembering her dream the first night she arrived at Ward's Pond. Katherine stared hard at Chester and Grace's pictures, positive that was who she'd seen in that boat.

"I wouldn't read that if I were you." She jumped. Charlie was propped against the entranceway, his jaw set, his eyes brooding. There was a pencil behind one ear, his cell phone pressed to the other, while a stack of papers filled his hands—with an apple from the kitchen balanced on top of everything. He slipped his phone in his pocket and took a step closer.

"Why? It's supposed to be a thorough account."

"Just because it's thorough doesn't mean it's true. It doesn't mean that book has all the answers. Even Craig Brandon admits that no one can tell for certain what happened to Grace, even though there was plenty of evidence against Chester. There were no eyewitness accounts and *neither* of them are coming back from the dead to prove otherwise.

The circumstantial evidence could be wrong. As for Chester, I've got to tell you. I really get sick of seeing a man condemned who can't defend himself. I've never been able to stomach that for anyone."

Katherine glanced down at the book again, only to glance back up and see that he had left. She looked in the kitchen and the dining area, but there was no sign. He'd probably gone back to his research. What she wouldn't give to have someone to talk to, someone to walk with her outside, like Charlie had the day before.

Pushing back her disappointment, she set the book down and pushed the screen door open, leaving the books, memories, dreams, and ghosts behind. Charlie was here on a mission and she had to accept that.

Her feet retraced the steps from her last trip around the pond. The shore called to her every day. It calmed her. *Strange.* Something about this place sent her feeling topsy-turvy only to settle her. Like Charlie…the moment he walked in her room during her nightmare and sat by her side, everything inside her went still.

Staring at her reflection in the water—completely unmoving at the moment—was like looking in a mirror. And then her vision shifted…and she saw the face of the young woman from her dream. *Grace.* Katherine closed her eyes tightly. Then she shook her head and looked again, breathing a sigh of relief. Only her own face stared back at her, a map she knew well. Maybe Charlie was right. She'd avoid that book the next time temptation whispered her name.

Backing away from the bank of the pond, she sat down on the bench overlooking the water, closed her eyes, and then pictured Charlie sitting beside her. That fall of hair that had an endearing habit of drifting in his way. The instant he pushed it aside and revealed the full power of eyes that were almost an electric blue—so bright they made it hard to breathe. Katherine sucked in deep, letting it go. *You're just getting out of one relationship. Do you really want to go down this road again?* This one, though…there was something different about this one.

Her eyes drifted shut again as a gentle breeze played with her hair and the sun warmed her face as she tilted it to the sky. Peaceful. It was so peaceful here. Easy to slip away.

"Katherine?! Where the hell are you?"

She tried to make herself smaller, curling up in a ball, wrapping her body in a blanket on the sofa in the dark. It was late—past midnight, perhaps—and Mike was just getting in after a night at the bar. His footsteps were heavy, moving through the rooms of their home. He stumbled and knocked into things, a few crashes and the drifting stench of alcohol telling her just how drunk he was. Did he literally go swimming in the stuff? She thought about slipping out the back door and going to the neighbors. It was best to distance herself on nights like this. Mike was a mean drunk.

"Katherine!" He cursed after ramming his knee into the end table, yelling at the offended joint and fumbling for the lamp. That was when she decided to make her move, rolling onto the floor as quietly as she could to scramble away. The glass door leading out to the deck was only a few feet away. If only she could make her way out without him hearing her…

The door made a quiet whoosh sound and she hit the deck, panting hard as the fear rose up and threatened to strangle her. A hand snagged her arm and whipped her around so hard she heard her neck crack. "Where do you think you're going?" Mike snarled at her, reeling her up against his chest.

What had she ever found attractive in this man? His blond hair was a wild tangle, his brown eyes bloodshot. Stubble covered his face, and it burned as he rubbed his cheek up against hers. The tears sprang to her eyes as his mouth clamped down on her lip hard enough to hurt. And then his free hand took hold of her breast. She thought he'd twist it off.

"Mike! Let go of me! You're hurting me and you're drunk! Let me go! Please!" Her voice rose in pitch. A bedroom light flicked on at their closest neighbor's house.

"Shut up, will ya? You'll wake up Herman and Eleanor over there!" His hand wrapped around her mouth. That scared her even more, making her feel entrapped. She took a chance and sank her teeth into his thumb, biting as hard

as she could. "Ouch! Bitch! HOW DARE YOU BITE THE HAND THAT FEEDS YOU?!"

With that, he pulled back and slapped her across the face before he gave her a hard shove. Maybe he didn't realize how close they were to the stairs.

Maybe he did.

Katherine lost her balance and tumbled down to the bottom, landing in a heap on the concrete patio. A stabbing pain ripped through her gut, followed by the sensation that her insides were spilling out of her. She looked down between her legs and watched a puddle of blood begin to spread beneath her. There was so much blood. She grabbed her stomach as her frantic screams pierced the night.

"Mind if I sit here?" She awoke with a jolt to find Charlie standing over her, wearing a crooked grin. After devoting hours to his work, he looked pale with smudges under his eyes. There was no way, no how she was going to heap more on his shoulders by telling him about her dream…or that perilous part of her past. While Katherine had agreed to be honest, that didn't mean she had to tell him everything.

"Please do. Tired of writing for a while?" The poor guy looked exhausted.

Charlie stretched his arms over his head. She could hear his back cracking, and she winced. "Yeah. I need a break. You can only bury yourself in that stuff for so long. After a while, you're afraid you'll never resurface!"

Katherine nodded and gave him a small smile, even as a chill ran through her. She pressed her palm to her stomach. After the dream, that terrible night, the agony and the fear were still so fresh. As if it happened yesterday. Looking out on the water, she pictured the woman of her nightmare the first night she arrived. *Grace.* Katherine might not know much about the Gillette-Brown murder, but she understood that feeling of carrying a child…and the loss…she knew what kind of pain that was. And she also knew what it could push a woman to do, driving her to the point of desperation.

Pushing aside dark thoughts, Katherine turned to the man beside her. Charlie had leaned forward, his elbows on his knees and his hands rubbing at his temples. She set her hand ever so lightly on the nape of his neck. "Step back from the research for a while; let it rest a few days. Sometimes the best way to understand someone is to walk in their shoes." Thinking about Grace Brown, a young woman who had carried a baby only to then lose that little one, Katherine fully understood. Yet their stories differed in one important way: Katherine had lived to tell her tale. Grace hadn't.

CHARLIE KNEW SHE WASN'T TELLING HIM SOMETHING. There were shadows in Katherine's eyes when he sat beside her on the bench by the pond, and she'd been trembling. What was she hiding? Lying on his bed, simply trying to catch a few hours of sleep, his mind kept going back to something she'd said. *"Sometimes the best way to understand someone is to walk in their shoes."*

How did he tell Katherine that he'd done more than share Gillette's shoes? Ever since he'd delved into this century-old murder—which was literally a cold case—Chester had been his shadow. Absolutely everywhere he turned.

4

NO MATTER HOW HARD HE TRIED, CHARLIE COULDN'T LET IT REST. He did his best to follow Katherine's advice. For a few days, he looked at maps, pinpointing where Chester Ellsworth Gillette had lived, where he was from, and who Chester had been before he was marked a murderer—while also trying to understand the man. He was tried, convicted, and then sent to death row until his life ended in the electric chair on March 30, 1908.

Charlie mulled over Chester's life story, looking back to his roots as a boy born on August 9, 1883 into a family of means out in Washington—only to have nothing when his parents gave it all up to be ministers for the Salvation Army. Wandering years had followed until Chester had his opportunity to make something of himself at Oberlin College, a prep school. Thanks to well-to-do uncles, he was headed down a promising path, but he didn't stay the course. He found himself nearly destitute again, working on the railroad and other odd jobs. His uncle, Noah H. Gillette, gave him one more chance to change his lot in life by giving him a job with prospects at the Gillette Skirt Factory. That was all well and good until Chester got Grace pregnant.

Charlie slammed his fist on his desk and laid his head down. None of it was any good. Chester's life, walking in his shoes, only suggested he was a selfish, frustrated young man who had lost everything one time too many. Getting a factory woman pregnant would have destroyed him, giving him all the more motive to get rid of the problem. *How can I defend the man?*

Wading his way through Craig Brandon's *Grace Brown's Love Letters*—including excerpts from her diary—only made matters worse. They might be muddled at times and inconsistent, but they painted a picture of a young woman who was in love, confused, and at wit's end about her unborn child, begging Chester time and time again to help her. And look where that got her. Charlie raked a hand through his hair and began to tug until his eyes smarted.

Grace…tell Grace. He sensed that a presence hovered over his shoulder. If Charlie looked out of the corner of his eye, he caught a dark-haired man in a suit. He sat up with a jerk.

Tell her what?! He swept all the papers off the table, sent them crashing to the floor, and whipped around. No one was there. Heart pounding, he raked a shaking hand through his hair and closed his eyes, his head starting to throb. *Tell her you were immature? That you were a self-centered jerk who couldn't stand by her and couldn't live up to your responsibilities?*

Charlie leaned forward and rested his elbows on the table, cradling his head in his hands. *Remember. He DID pay. With his life. A life for a life.* That didn't make it right; it didn't fix what Chester Gillette did. The fact that the man shared his blood didn't make it any easier.

Tell Grace. Charlie leapt to his feet. "Just leave me the hell alone, why don't you?" Belatedly, he heard a tentative knock on his door.

"Sorry. I'll…I'll let you be," a muffled voice said softly, on the verge of tears. *Katherine!*

He rushed to the door, flinging it open. "Katherine! Sorry, I wasn't talking to you. I tend to get a bit carried away when I'm researching…I talk to myself, you know?"

Katherine slid him a smile and then stepped inside, glancing around his room. "I think you need a break. When you didn't come to breakfast, I figured this…" she said and waved vaguely to his piles of papers, "…was what happened. Here's a breakfast sandwich from Eva and a thermos of coffee. I'm springing you and we are going to the Violet Festival. No arguments." She pressed a finger between his shoulder blades. "Go get gussied up."

He laughed and impulsively leaned in to skim her cheek with his lips. She looked mesmerizing—done up in a violet-colored dress, surrounding him with some heavenly scent that couldn't be ignored. A wreath of violets was entwined in her dark hair, and it was pulled up in a French braid, forming what resembled a crown. Incredible. Just one stare into those eyes that held the green of summer and he wouldn't ever want to move again.

Charlie forced himself to go to the bathroom, glanced in the mirror, and saw Chester for an instant. He gripped the sink so hard his knuckles stood out. *Damn it, Chester. Enough!*

He splashed water on his face and the image disappeared. It was probably just a figment of an extremely overactive, overtired imagination that had already been working this case for six weeks. If he spent much more time immersed in the past, his mind would come unhinged.

Charlie checked his clothes. *A white T-shirt, thankfully clean.* The shirt was covered by a button-down in plaid with blue and white stripes. *Dark jeans. All right.* He swept a hand through his hair and put his game face on, only to practically lose it when Katherine grazed his jaw with her lips when he stepped out. Her breath smelled like spearmint. *Was Chester as enchanted by Grace as you are by Katherine, Charlie?* He mentally stomped on that question and offered Katherine his hand.

Charlie and Katherine ambled, slowly, heading up Van Buren Street to the main drag in Dolgeville. The village was like a young girl headed to the prom, dressed in her best, decked out with purple ribbons and an explosion of violets everywhere. It was an annual celebration that celebrated the violets that were native to a greenhouse in the area, dating back to the '50s—not to mention their proud heritage that could be credited to Alfred Dolge. A parade, street play, and vendors provided plenty of distractions, ushering in the hustle and bustle.

After browsing in a few of the stands, Katherine lit up like a kid when she saw the cart with cotton candy, fried dough, and candy apples included in the lineup. "We have to have everything," she told Charlie, tugging him across the street.

Her enthusiasm was contagious. He willingly obliged, digging out his wallet and buying one of each treat. "Do you think it's all right if we start out by sharing? I'll buy you more if you want it."

Katherine looped her arms around his neck and kissed him, her lips tasting like the cotton candy that she had just sampled. It was almost too sweet to handle. "Perfect. Let's go find a place to sit down and munch."

She found them a bench along the sidewalk—prime seating with a wondrous view for all the festivities. When all the sweets were gone, Charlie made a return trip to the vendor for the largest strawberry lemonade they had, plus a box of popcorn. The kind with red-and-white stripes that made him think of going to the circus while he was growing up.

Walking back to Katherine, a wave of nostalgia rolled over him. To be a kid again. Young and innocent, with no ghost stories from his past to torment him. Charlie swallowed hard and stumbled to a halt as a vision of Chester and a young, lost girl appeared in front of him. In the middle of a lake. In the dark on a hot summer night. In a rowboat that began to rock…

"Oh, no you don't. You're thinking about that story again. It's been over for more than a century, Charlie. It can wait another day. Those people have been dead and gone for more than a hundred years. You and I are very much alive." She took the drink and grabbed his hand, leading him back to their bench, making his heart skitter at her touch. Her scent. The flash of her eyes. Her…everything. "Listen! I can hear the band playing! The parade is on its way!"

A bubble of happiness rose up inside him, one large enough to push away the sadness and darkness that had plagued him since he took on this book—a project meant to set the record straight. Charlie didn't question it. He sat back, his arm wrapped around Katherine's shoulders, giving himself up to the warm weight of her as she leaned against him. She was right. For today, Chester and Grace would have to wait. The land of the living was calling to him.

As soon as the parade was over, a street band began to play old favorites like "Long, Tall Sally," and "Brown-Eyed Girl." Katherine jumped up and pulled Charlie into a dance, her arms fitting where they should be, right around his neck. Her lips pressed to his and his hands settled on her hips as they began to sway. He was here. Right now. Leaving no room in his mind for anything except *this* woman and no one else.

THEY DANCED UNTIL SHE RAN OUT OF BREATH AND HER FEET WERE TIRED. Katherine knew she should've worn something more comfortable than her high-heeled boots, but they were cute, and Charlie was in serious need of a distraction.

"Woo! I'm hot now and dry as a bone. I'll run up and get us another lemonade…unless you want a hard cider?" Charlie shook his head, his face flushed from the dancing. Or was it from her? Whatever the reason, it was good to see those blue eyes shining brighter than the cloudless sky unfurling over their heads like a giant flag waving in the breeze.

He held her hand all the way back to the cart, and Katherine was just fine with that. Charlie didn't ever have to let go. She laid her money down for their lemonade and poked two straws in the cup, holding it up to give him a sip. They both took a long draw at the same time, knocking foreheads as they did.

"Oof! Gotta be careful there. You all right?" he asked, laughing.

Katherine stood on tiptoe and kissed the red mark on his head. "I'm fine. You?"

"Let me return the favor." He leaned in, kissing her forehead. His hand came up to skim along her jaw before he cupped her face and set his lips on hers.

Katherine's heart started to do a mad dance and her stomach tightened. Her breath came out in a rush and she looked up at him when a tall blond man in the distance made her gasp. She grabbed Charlie's hand and pulled him behind a stand of trees, her back pressed up against it with her eyes closed. She took a second to catch her breath and then peered cautiously around the side only to wilt in relief. "Whew. I thought I saw Mike, my ex."

Charlie's jaw tightened, his eyes growing dark as he studied her intently. "Is there some kind of trouble with this Mike that you're not telling me about?"

She shook her head. "No…it's just I have a restraining order and he shouldn't be near me. I didn't tell him where I was going…" Katherine began to fumble with her words. She knew how bad it sounded.

"Katherine, a restraining order? Keeping secrets? Has this guy hurt you?" The storm clouds were brewing with thunder in his eyes. His body was tense, his hands curling into formidable fists as if ready to step into the boxing ring.

She touched his arm, trying to put on a brave front, but failed miserably as the tears rose to the surface. "Yes…yes he did. Once, but once was one time too many. I filed for divorce right away. He hasn't been very cooperative, but the process is underway. I've distanced myself to make it easier. I really don't think he'd hurt me again. It's only when he drinks…but I'm not willing to find out. Mike broke my trust the day he laid a hand on me in anger."

Charlie paced back and forth, hands on his hips. "I don't like it, Katherine. I want to see his picture. Show me so I can spot him, in case he does show up."

She fumbled with her phone, pulled it out, and then flicked through until she found her wedding picture. She hadn't had the heart to delete it. Katherine thought she had the fairytale back then. He'd seemed so good for her. *Too good to be true.* "That's him, Michael Graciano."

Charlie nodded and wrapped an arm around her. He scanned the milling crowds, a line forming between his eyes, searching for the man in her phone. No one fit the description. He drew Katherine in closer, becoming her shield. "I don't want you to be scared anymore. If I have anything to say about it, he'll never touch you again." She'd already made that vow. The tall, strong wall of a man at her side made it even easier to keep it.

SITTING IN THE PARLOR, FIDDLING WITH HER PHONE, Katherine struggled to resist the temptation to look up Mike's Facebook page. To pinpoint his location. She lived in fear that he was getting closer—that somehow, no matter how careful she had been, the man would find her and destroy her newfound, fragile peace.

Squashing her anxious thoughts, she locked them away in the back of her mind and started googling Chester Gillette and Grace Brown, a good distraction if ever there was one. Every single source condemned Gillette and found him guilty except for his own journal—although there was no definitive evidence. Sighing, she closed her eyes for an instant when a creepy sensation had her sitting up straight on the sofa, the hairs on her arms standing on end.

Someone was watching her. Her throat began to close up, her heart thumping loud enough to thrum in her ears. Katherine always feared the shadow looming behind her would be her ex-husband. Steeling herself, she glanced over her shoulder. A dark-haired woman, dressed in white, with unspeakably sad eyes stood at the window, looking in. With trembling hands, Katherine skimmed through photos on her phone, stopping at a picture of Grace. The same face as the woman in the window gazed up at her. Katherine swallowed hard and turned around. The mysterious visitor was gone.

Unable to believe what she saw, Katherine typed in "Grace Mae Brown." The articles and images filled web page after web page, starting with the time of Grace's death and ending only a few years ago when women reported seeing her ghost on Big Moose Lake, becoming a focus of *Unsolved Mysteries*, the popular television show. Bombarded with too much information and overwhelmed by her spiritual encounter, Katherine put the phone down and then pressed her hands to her eyes. Her head was throbbing.

A hand touched her shoulder, making her jump. Charlie stood over her, pale and tired. Katherine didn't like the look of him. Pushing aside her own fears, she took his hand and pulled him down beside her on the sofa. Charlie slid closer to give her a kiss, his face twisting when he caught the pictures on her phone. "It's hard to leave it alone, isn't it?"

"I'm afraid so. It's got me hooked, too…but not like you." It didn't seem like the right time to tell him about her ghostly visitor. Or the dream. *It's probably just your imagination.*

"Yeah…I've been living, eating, sleeping, and breathing this story for nearly two months. I've even got a DVD of *A Place in the Sun*, because it might give me insight, even if it is a fictional retelling inspired by the case." Charlie leaned back and rested an arm over his eyes. Katherine suspected he could fall asleep right there.

"I've heard about that classic. Why don't we make it a movie night and watch together? I might notice something that you don't since I'm not so close to the case. There's only one rule. Don't take it too seriously. Remember that this is Hollywood's version of the story, and you know how they exaggerate! What do you say, Charlie? Popcorn, soda; some cuddles and laughs. Good, clean fun."

HE COULDN'T TELL HER NO and to be completely honest, Charlie couldn't stand the thought of another night locked up alone with his thoughts, the Gillette-Brown murder, and Chester's shadow hovering nearby at all hours. But the movie? That didn't count. It was Elizabeth Taylor, Shelley Winters, and Montgomery Clift. Actors from Hollywood's heyday, putting on the glitz with their star power. There was no way that they could do an authentic account of what happened between Grace and Chester. Watching a movie with Katherine? That would be a badly needed escape. Charlie didn't care what they watched. Maybe he'd even get out of his head.

There was no denying that Katherine was a powerful attraction. Look up the word "aphrodisiac" and her picture would be next to the definition, he mused. With every passing day, he had more opportunities to see her...and was having a hard time getting through a day without her.

Yet he had his doubts. He'd never been serious about a girl before. Having a murderer in his blood did that to a guy. *Accused murderer*, the defense attorney in his brain shouted out.

Tried and convicted. Fried, the devil's advocate in the form of the prosecutor wrangled back internally. All of that didn't matter when he became caught up watching Katherine. The way she moved, the tilt of her head, and those creek-water eyes. The soft, musical tone of her voice—her curves. There was a light about her that drew him in, made him want to knock down all the barriers he'd erected...and it terrified him. What if there was something intrinsically wrong with him, passed down in his genetic code, the same something that made Chester snap?

Charlie shuddered and doused his face in cold water. If he could put out the thoughts that singed his mind, he'd not hesitate. He stared at his reflection in the mirror and reminded himself. *You are NOT Chester.*

That night, while preparing for their movie, Charlie treated it like a date. He stood under the shower for a long time, the steaming water beating down on his skull, struggling to clear his head of all things Grace and Chester. Tonight, he only wanted to think about Katherine.

Standing in his room, he surveyed the wreckage as he quickly dressed in jeans and a short-sleeved button-down. The place was a mess. He'd insisted Eva stop coming in to tidy up or she'd be scandalized. He was a big boy; he could clean up after himself. Charlie nodded curtly. "Right. Starting now."

He began with his desk, a mountain of papers about to teeter on to the floor. Methodically, he filed anything important. Ruthlessly, he tossed the rest into the garbage. Before long, Charlie could actually see a desk again. He made his bed, straightened up the bathroom, and gathered up the water bottles scattered throughout the room. A quick spray of air freshener with the windows pulled wide open and it would pass inspection.

Finally, Charlie plumped the pillows and propped them up to create the perfect viewing spot. *For the movie*, he reminded himself. *You'll only be watching her, and you know it.* Eva willingly helped him on his mission, making a heaping bowl of buttery, salty popcorn and ice cream sodas. Everything was ready, so why were his palms sweating like it was prom night?

Katherine was punctual, tapping on his door at seven. She kissed him lightly and slipped off her shoes, sliding onto the bed. She'd dressed in jeans and a navy T-shirt—nothing racy, but it didn't matter. The gorgeous girl could wear a burlap sack and it would send his body into overdrive.

While waiting for the movie to start, she spotted *An American Tragedy* on the nightstand with CliffsNotes next to it. She picked it up and made a big show of lifting it. "Whoa. Pretty hefty. I can see why you'd take a shortcut."

He shrugged. "It's just a novel, anyway, not the actual case…although Theodore Dreiser drew heavily from the true story. Some would even say he cut and pasted certain parts from the newspapers and Grace's letters, only to slap it all in his manuscript." Charlie held out his hand for the book, which he shoved in his briefcase. "I didn't even want to read it, but everyone who's anyone told me I had to, or I'd be missing out. It's just the more I think about it, I don't want to know what other people wrote about Chester and Grace. I'm looking for a fresh perspective through new eyes. *My* eyes."

Grace took his hand. "Stick to your guns." She was warm and smelled so sweet. Charlie couldn't stand it anymore. Look, but don't touch was not possible with Katherine Grace Brown. He set the remote down and pressed his lips to hers. He felt himself sliding deeper and deeper every time he came near her. A little more of Katherine and he wouldn't be able to remember who Grace and Chester were. Or why he was even here…yet it didn't matter.

The movie began, making them both laugh self-consciously. Charlie paused it long enough to make sure they were situated, side by side with their backs propped up by pillows and the bowl of popcorn conveniently placed between them. Their focus shifted to the movie; at least it looked that way.

But Charlie found himself paying more attention to Katherine than *A Place in the Sun*, observing the way her hair rested on her cheek and the crease between her eyes when she was thinking hard. At some point, she ended up on his lap, thoroughly kissing him to oblivion.

They pulled away, suddenly shy, looking away from each other. Chuckling nervously, Charlie forced himself to follow the movie until it nearly made his heart stop like he'd run into a brick wall. It was the murder scene. He almost jumped up, calling, "No, Grace!" before she fell overboard, but he stopped himself. *It's a movie. Just a movie.*

Quiet fell between them for the rest of the film. At the end, when Montgomery Clift was sent to the electric chair, Charlie could hear Katherine sniffling, dabbing at her eyes as the tears slid down her face.

Charlie turned off the television and took her hand. "Maybe Grace really did fall…or maybe she jumped. Her letters talked about suicide."

Katherine stood up quickly, her arms crossed over her chest, upset. "Grace didn't kill herself, Charlie. Don't ask me how I know—I just know. She had a trunk filled to the brim with clothes. I think she expected Chester to do right by her and get her to the home for unwed mothers…and I think he killed her because *he* didn't want the complications. Get your head out of your pile of books and papers so you can see what everyone else already has." Tension crackled between them. "I'd better go now. It's much too late and I'm really tired. I'm saying things I'll probably regret later. Thanks for the movie night."

The door slammed behind her on the way out. She didn't even say good night. *Thanks for nothing.*

5

CHARLIE LEANED HIS BACK AGAINST HIS DOOR and banged his fist on his leg. What was wrong with him…showing her a movie like that in a house that was steeped in references to a real-life murder, of all things? *Way to go, Charlie. You really know how to impress a girl! What will you do for an encore? Take her on a tour of death row?*

Grumbling, he decided to apologize to Katherine, though it was past midnight. He yanked the door open and took the few steps to cross the hall. The irony and déjà vu hit him. *It's quite like the night you two first met.* Charlie raised his hand to knock, pulling up short when he heard her voice rising. She must've been talking to someone on the phone. *Or her own personal ghost.*

"I thought we weren't going to do this, Mike. We said it's over and done, no more fighting. You want the grill? Fine, go get the damned grill out of the storage unit. Take anything you want. Load the entire unit on a tractor trailer and tow it outta there. I don't care. I'll call the manager and tell him to let you in. Just leave me alone. Do you hear me? Leave me the hell alone!"

The sound of crying came next, muffled as if she was burying her face in a pillow. Charlie's stomach twisted into knots and he turned around, slipping quietly back inside his room. If there was one thing he couldn't tolerate, it was a crying woman, but to go in there now would be an intrusion.

He stretched out on his bed, not even bothering to get undressed, his eyes trained on the ceiling. He was just unable to sleep. His head was too full with the movie, theories about Grace's death, and Katherine—simply torn between the urge to argue with her about his gut instincts concerning the case and the need to comfort her.

When his eyes burned from staring into the darkness without blinking and he couldn't stand to do nothing a second longer, he lunged from his bed and started digging into the past again, hoping against hope that *something* new would turn up. Something to exonerate Chester or seal his fate, leaving no more doubts in anyone's mind. For the sake of the Brown family. The Gillette family. And Charlie's mother. For Charlie as well, because this had stopped being purely academic a long time ago. This was so personal, it jabbed at him like a stake through the heart.

"HELLO?" CHARLIE'S VOICE WAS HOARSE, as if he'd inhaled smoke. His mouth was as dry as he imagined the bottom of an ashtray would be, his eyes nearly swollen shut from lack of sleep and staring at words until they began to dance, blur, and shift on the screen. He'd finally dropped off into the sleep of the dead at dawn. Squinting, he looked at his phone and managed to make out the time. It was now eight A.M. "Hello?" He tried again. *If this is a telemarketer, so help me…*

"Good morning, Mr. Baxter? I do hope it's not too early. You know what they say. The early bird gets the worm!" The lady was way too chipper for this hour of the morning, especially when he felt like he had a hangover. He mumbled something unintelligible. The cheery caller plowed on as if she hadn't heard him.

"This is Irene Muldowney over at the Dolgeville Library. You asked me to look for the original newspapers from the Gillette-Brown case.

Quite a job, I tell you. Quite a job. I was digging through those boxes for days. I just about gave up when eureka—I hit the jackpot! All of them have been found—everything from the local papers, plus the *New York Times!*"

Charlie's brain cleared like a fog burning off after a summer storm on a hazy night. He rose up fast, his heart racing as his feet hit the floor. "When can I come look at them, Ms. Muldowney?"

Laughter—sweet and young as a schoolgirl's—filled his ears even though Charlie imagined the librarian to be an older woman. "My, aren't we the eager beaver? Come in whenever you'd like. It's Sunday and I'm usually closed today. I figured you would need a while. I've already taken the liberty of copying them all for you as well to take with you when you go. I thought you'd like to get your hands on the real McCoy. I'll be waiting for you. I'm looking forward to meeting a fellow seeker of the truth." With those cryptic words, the line disconnected.

Charlie took a five-minute shower, blasting the water on cold to shake off the last traces of sleepiness that threatened to muddy his thinking. Throwing on some jeans and a white button-down shirt, he decided a quick run of a comb through his hair was the best he could manage that morning. *No time to shave. Five o'clock shadow will have to do.*

Charlie poked his sunglasses in his pocket, grabbed his briefcase, and then headed downstairs, half-dreading a confrontation with Katherine. He nearly sagged against the doorjamb to find an empty dining room and parlor upon his arrival. She was probably sleeping in, recovering after a rough night.

Eva stuck her head out from the kitchen. "Morning, Charlie! What would you like on this fine June day on the brink of summer?"

He winced and rubbed his temple. People were entirely too enthusiastic around here. "Could I just have coffee in a thermos, Eva? I'm on the fly this morning."

"Will do. Be back in a jiff."

True to her word, she met him as he reached the porch. She handed over the cup, tilting her head when she got a close-up of his face. Her finger came up to wag at him, and he couldn't blame her. The mirror had spoken loud and clear, revealing the bruise-like smudges under his eyes and pale skin of someone who had been within four walls for far too long.

"Charlie, you should take yourself back upstairs to bed after I put some real food in your stomach." Eva poked his side in emphasis only to *tsk-tsk*. "You're spreading yourself too thin, and this story isn't worth it."

After staying at the bed and breakfast for two months or so, he'd started to feel at home; Eva was like a sister. He stepped in and gave her a quick hug. "I'll take you up on your advice the next time. The librarian has found a gold mine and I don't want to keep her waiting. I'm going to walk if anyone wonders why my car is here."

He slipped away before she could argue with him any further. Charlie had the need to move, breathe in the fresh air, and get some exposure to direct sunlight once again. Maybe a good walk would help him to distance himself a bit from Chester and Grace. *How about Katherine?*

His jaw set at that one, and his shoulders became so tight he had to make a conscious effort to loosen up. Being tangled up with Katherine was one mess that he really didn't know how to undo—just a beautiful mess. Charlie's mind turned to the many moments he'd studied her, creating mental images that he could carry with him always, no matter which way his research led him or if she possibly dropped out of his life.

The Dolgeville library brought him to a halt in surprise. Somehow, he'd arrived at the small, unassuming building without even realizing it, as his thoughts had been terribly occupied. The door swung open and a woman stood in the entranceway, shattering all his illusions about the matronly, old caretaker of the realm of books in every small town in America. "Well, don't just stand there gawking all day! Come on in!"

Irene Muldowney might have been a bit older than his twenty-eight years, but not by much. She was dressed like a girl out of the fifties, with her jet-black hair in sweeping curls, held back by a red bandana that was tied in a knot on one side to match the splash of crimson lipstick on her mouth. She had eyes of blue—like the ocean or the marbles he'd had in a bag as a kid, pale and somehow bottomless—surrounded by glasses with black, pointy frames. Her jeans were rolled up to the calf, her white blouse was knotted at the waist, and a red sweater completed the ensemble. She perched on high heels of red with white polka dots...and she was snapping gum. Charlie stood glued to his patch of sidewalk like the Tin Man when he rusted solid in *The Wizard of Oz*.

"Mr. Baxter, I don't think that I can physically move you into this establishment, but I will give it a go. One never knows what one can accomplish until one tries." She took one step forward, giving him a wink.

That was enough to jolt him into action, so he immediately jogged up the steps and took her hand. "I'm sorry, Ms. Muldowney. You're just..."

"Not what you expected. For anyone who hasn't been in since I took over the helm or those who talk with me on the phone, you would not be the first. I'm a—what do they say?—throwback. Blame it on my grandmother who raised me. She was the last librarian and held the post for sixty years. I figured I'd keep her spirit alive and carry on her traditions."

It was hard keeping up with the woman. She moved remarkably fast on those neck-breaker heels, but her tongue moved even faster. Considering that Charlie's mental capabilities were running pretty slow, it was going to be a challenge. He took a good swig of his coffee, burning his mouth in the process. Now that gave his brain a jump-start. "I'm sorry for your loss."

49

She turned and patted his shoulder. "Nana Becker didn't die. She just decided it was time to pass the torch. You'll have to meet her sometime."

With that, the young woman stopped in her tracks and swung around, offering him her hand. Her red nails were incredibly long and had black polka dots. *Like ladybugs.* Charlie suspected he needed a good night's sleep, because it was a struggle to listen to her words while staring at the nails...and everything else. "Pardon my manners! I haven't officially introduced myself. I'm Irene Muldowney, a Dolgeville girl born and raised. You may call me Irene."

He couldn't help but pull out a smile. The girl was so darned cheerful and downright enthusiastic. "I'm Charlie Baxter. Please call me Charlie." He shook her hand and was nearly blinded by her smile.

A few steps farther, she gave him a deep bow. "Here you are. All the tables in this room have the original newspapers spread out for your perusal. I've gathered the copies in this manila folder for you—which is yours to keep. I'm going to leave you to your privacy, but if you need anything—anything at all—my office is in the back. I'll be doing my best to get through a stack of new books that I'm considering for our collection. I try to at least get a sample before I put anything on our shelves so that I know what this place holds. You know what that means, don't you?" She waited expectantly. When he shook his head, Irene laughed. "That I'll have job security until my rocking-chair years with all the books that I have to read."

Her heels tapped off down the hallway, leaving him to his own devices. Charlie let out the breath he didn't know had been on hold. *Man, that woman can talk!* With his head still spinning, he drank the rest of his coffee and got down to business.

He had to give Irene credit. She'd been methodical and thorough, laying everything out in chronological order, arranging articles from the local area and national coverage side by side, making sure that nothing was missed. Digging his heels in for the long haul, Charlie completely lost track of time.

Headlines shouted out at him, mostly cries of outrage about the heartless Gillette, demonizing him in many ways, painting a picture of Grace as a poor innocent lamb of a girl.

Mystery in Girl's Death: Body Found in Adirondack Lake — Man Companion Missing, from the *New York Times,* July 14, 1906

Grace Brown a Suicide, Says Gillette at Trial, New York Times, originally published: November 29, 1906

Grace Brown's Letters Stir Audience to Tears, New York Times, November 20, 1906

Charlie couldn't believe how quickly the trial moved along, some articles beginning with coverage when it started in the Herkimer County Courthouse on November 11, 1906. By December 4th, Chester was found guilty. What a difference from the interminable court cases of modern day. Charlie could still remember the circus surrounding the OJ Simpson trial. His mother had told him all about that travesty.

Hungrily, his eyes devoured every article. To read what was written at the time, even if it was sensationalized, made the story seem so real. As if he were living it himself. Taking him from the shocking beginning...to the dreaded end. One blurb from the *New York Times* made it hard to breathe. It read,

"ALBANY, March 28. — The life of Chester Gillette lies in the hands of Gov. Hughes. What is said to be newly discovered evidence was submitted to the Governor today, and between now and tomorrow night, he will decide whether or not he will reprieve the young man, who without his interference would die in the electric chair at Auburn Prison, probably in the dawn of next Monday morning." The date tripped Charlie up. Only two days before Chester's execution in 1908.

So close. Gillette had nearly been spared. Charlie bowed his head only to straighten up as he felt a presence at his side. He closed his eyes and swallowed hard, taking a deep breath in and then steeling himself. A quick peek and he caught a glimpse of Chester, giving him a start. He'd never get used to these sudden appearances, although he suspected his relative was always with him, whether Gillette chose to make his presence known or not. Chester raised one hand, pointing to the last table and the only paper that had yet to be touched.

Charlie suddenly felt cold. To the bone. As if he'd stepped out into a blizzard without anything but his underwear and was left there to freeze into a solid block of ice. He didn't want to look at the article. Somehow, his heart already knew what it would say. His eyes traveled straight to the source. The *Los Angeles Herald*. Volume 35. Number 181. March 31, 1908.

No. I don't want to read it. He felt a hand on his shoulder. Steadying him. Comforting him, but insistent, urging him on. Charlie opened his eyes and forced himself to read the final headline that put a period on Chester Gillette's life where so many exclamation marks and question marks had been before.

IN SHADOW OF DEATH HE CONFESSES
GILLETTE SIGNS STATEMENT TO YOUNG MEN
PAYS PENALTY FOR DEED IN ELECTRIC CHAIR . i Walks Firmly and Briskly to His Doom and Accepts His Fate - Without Murmur or Question By Associated Press. AUBURN N. Y. March 30.—Chester E. Gillette today paid the full penalty for the brutal murder of Grace Brown. He went to his death in the electric chair at Auburn prison without a sign of weakness and with the same lack of emotion which has characterized him from the day he was arrested charged with the crime.
Gillette appeared to have been fully reconciled to his fate, and in a statement given out by his spiritual advisers immediately after the execution, it is indicated that he had made a confession of his guilt. This statement was signed by the Rev. Henry McIlravy of Little Falls and the Rev. Cordello Herrick, the prison chaplain who attended Gillette since he-had been in the death cell at the prison. It was as follows:
"Because our relationship with Chester Gillette was privileged, we do not deem it wise to make a detailed statement and simply wish to say that no legal mistake was made in his electrocution."

Gillette himself, so far as the public was concerned, never admitted his crime. His last words, in the form of a statement' which he had prepared with painstaking care, were made public after he had been put to death. In this statement Gillette implored young men to lead Christian lives. Any fear which the prison officials may have entertained that Gillette's remarkable composure would desert him at the last moment was quickly dispelled when he stepped from his cell to the corridor leading to the death chamber. His step was firm and strong, and he walked rapidly toward the Instrument of death. Not even by the quiver of an eyelid did he betray the least sign of emotion and at no stage did he require assistance from the keepers and his spiritual advisers who accompanied him in his last walk. He seated himself in the chair, the straps and electrodes were placed and within two minutes Gillette had been officially pronounced dead. The electrocution was the most successful that ever took place in the local prison. But one contact was required to carry the mandates of the law into effect, and when that was over, the murderer of Grace Brown had paid the penalty of his crime. 'Electrocution Is Quick.' The electrocution was marked throughout with celerity. The man was declared dead by the officials at 6:18.

Just like that. A life snuffed out, without hesitation. A young man's future ended in such a violent manner. Was justice served? Was the legal system truly any better than whatever happened between Gillette and Grace on that lonely boat on Big Moose Lake? How had Chester been able to walk to meet his death without fear? There were simply too many questions. Charlie's fingers splayed across the page as he pinched the bridge of his nose, his body beginning to sway.

"Oh, my. This will never do." Irene ducked under his shoulder and led him to a chair, where Charlie bent forward and cupped his head in his hands. For a moment, the librarian lingered, her hand on his before she moved away, returning with a tall glass of lemonade and a plate heaped with food. "You drink that. You've got to be parched, and I think you need something other than coffee. Your nerves are quite frayed already, I suspect. Then I want you to eat something. I could hear your stomach growling from across the room even though you didn't seem to notice."

Charlie thanked her and picked up the lemonade first. He didn't realize just how strong his thirst was until the glass was drained within seconds. Sheepishly, he nodded when asked for a refill. Irene sat beside him and waited patiently while he took a few more swallows and regained his composure. "Thank you. That tastes really good. I can't take your sandwich."

Irene waved off his objections. "We'll split it, all right? My eyes were bigger than my stomach this morning." She handed him half of a turkey club and started in on hers. Not wishing to be rude, he took a bite. Suddenly ravenous, Charlie quickly scarfed down his portion. Laughing, Irene sliced off the uneaten section of hers and handed it over. "Don't worry. I have another one in the fridge for later."

They sat in companionable silence, munching on chips and sipping lemonade until everything was polished off. Irene nodded in approval. "Better now? I don't know if you realize, but it's already past three. Heading on toward dinnertime. Small wonder you were so hungry. You were really lost in your work. If you don't mind my asking, what has you so fired up about the Gillette-Brown murder case? It's old news. You'll find a few die-hard scholars who are curious like me, but most have moved on."

Charlie leaned back in his chair and rested a hand on his stomach. He'd eaten too much, too fast. Letting out a sigh, he decided to be up front with the librarian. "I'm a distant relative to Chester—on my mother's side of the family."

Irene's eyes widened as she leaned forward, propping her chin on one hand. "Hmm. That *would* stick in your craw, wouldn't it? A case like that with family ties. So, you're looking for any stones that have been unturned—a different angle, perhaps?"

Charlie shrugged. "Maybe. Heck, I don't know." Unable to sit any longer, he stood up abruptly and began to pace, running a hand through his hair in frustration. "It's like looking for a needle in a haystack that's mammoth enough to cover the country. I mean...all of it—every one of these papers—condemned Chester before he even went to trial. It's as if everyone made up their minds right from the start. Whatever happened to innocent until proven guilty?"

He moved to the table with the final article in the paper and smacked his hand down. "Even when he went to the chair, calmly and without protest, can't you just hear them gloating smugly, 'Guilty as charged!' What the hell is that supposed to mean from the spiritual advisors, that there was no legal mistake in his electrocution? They'd have to say that, wouldn't they? If only to be able to live with themselves. Perhaps Chester just admitted he did wrong by Grace—getting involved with her, getting her pregnant, and then taking her out on the boat…he played a part in her death. That doesn't mean he killed her!"

Charlie stopped and bowed his head. His search in the library hadn't given him any leads. *You're right back where you started.* All the while, he felt Chester's somber presence, hovering nearby. Watching. Waiting. Waiting for what? *If there's something I don't see, show me the way, damn it!*

Irene spoke softly, breaking into his inner war. She was still seated behind Charlie. She'd been silent the entire time, allowing him to get what he had to say off his chest. "You know, all you heard about was the scandal and outrage that came up about Gillette's case. They went after Chester like he was the devil himself. It reminds me of the Salem Witch Trial, for Pete's sake. *No one* believed it could've been an accident. What was that business about a tennis racket? So a witness saw the racket strapped to his case. It was all part of their cover story, heading off on a wedding trip. They were on a lake. The racket may have fallen off the boat. But nothing proves it was Chester's murder weapon. It was circumstantial. So much of the evidence was circumstantial. Even the governor appeared to be torn about the matter."

Charlie grimaced. The whole thing made him feel sick to his stomach. "I'm sure he didn't give that stay of execution because the public wanted someone to pay the ultimate price. They needed a scapegoat. Guilty or not, Chester got the bullseye!"

Irene's forehead creased as she digested his tirade. "The other thing that really bothers me is this: if Grace was so innocent…such a good, sweet girl, why'd she sleep with Chester before they were married? She was old enough to understand what could happen and *had* to know that sleeping with the boss's nephew was taboo. *None* of these articles brought up that undeniable truth—or the fact that Grace was a consenting adult. Her letters prove she was willing. Chester didn't force himself on her."

The chair scraped behind Charlie as the librarian stood up and moved to one of the papers. On the other side of the room, he could see Chester propped against the wall, listening silently with that solemn expression that went with him everywhere. Whether his eyes were open or closed, Charlie saw his ancestor. "Here's another thing to think about. Those letters that George Ward presented as evidence?" She picked up one of the articles and waved it in the air. "Threatening to kill herself…how she couldn't possibly tell Mama…telling Chester no one had ever been so good to her…trying to guilt him into marrying her. What if that was her goal all along when she first started sleeping with him? Just a thought. No matter what, I'm glad you're looking into this case again. With your connections to the family, you've got a reason to dig deeper. Back then, I believe Judge Ward only scratched the surface, a hundred pieces of evidence notwithstanding. I think you'll be the one to find out the truth, good or bad." She paused and forced a smile. "Now I think it's time you went out in the daylight and took a breather. You're looking peaked. You've had enough of murder and mayhem for one day."

"Thank you for all you've done, Irene. You truly went above and beyond. I'll bring you an autographed copy when the book's all done." He gathered everything in his briefcase, including the folder filled with copies of the newspaper articles, and then shook her hand. It was getting hard to breathe with the walls of the library closing in on him. He had to get out.

Charlie hit the sidewalk and went halfway down the block before he dropped down on a bench. He pressed his hands to his temples and began to rub at them—hard. So muddled. So uncertain of everything. He didn't think that Grace tried to trap Chester, that she could be conniving. Most likely, she just got swept away. He was a nice-looking young man and also the owner's nephew. She must've been impressed that he even showed an interest. No, Grace shouldn't have slept with him, but Chester never should've started anything with *her*. Charlie's relative had failed to live up to the high moral standards of the time— or his upbringing, for that matter. He'd started something that never should have happened and look how tragically it ended. *You play with fire, you're gonna get burned.*

Grace. Tell Grace. Such anguish in the voice whispering in his ear. Charlie came up fast and caught Chester on the edge of his line of sight. Turning to look at him head-on, he realized there was nothing there. Charlie pulled himself up to his feet and gritted his teeth. "Enough of this," he muttered under his breath. "I need more than a break. I *need* a drink." He set his destination for Arthur's and found himself a spot at the bar. The first tall beer went down fast. For once, Chester stayed outside.

6

SHE FELT LIKE A FLY TRAPPED IN A SPIDER'S WEB. If Michael Graciano couldn't find her, he'd bring her to him. "Not if I can help it," she growled, sitting in her car and banging her hands on the wheel.

Katherine drove a few blocks away from the bed and breakfast, pulling over into a convenience store parking lot. She pulled out her cell and dialed the storage facility in Utica, tapping her finger on the dash while she waited. She'd picked the first place that came up online once the house sold and all of her stuff was packed up, then drove a U-Haul van by herself like a bat out of hell, putting distance between Syracuse and all things Michael. It was a small miracle that a police officer hadn't pulled her over or she hadn't had an accident—with the way her sobbing made it nearly impossible to see.

And the manager was no help whatsoever. "Sorry, Ms. Brown. *You* have to be here. You're the only name on the unit and it's in your contract, to make sure it really is you, you know? It's for your security. I seem to remember that you wanted it that way when you signed on the dotted line."

With a forceful push of the button, Katherine hung up. She resisted the strong urge to pound the phone against the dashboard. Hanging up on a cell phone was not nearly as satisfying as slamming a receiver down, like the old black phone on Nana's farm with a rotary dial.

She called her mother next. "Mom, will you go with my spare key for the storage unit and open it for Mike? He wants the grill and I don't want to see him…yes, Mom, I know. Yes, I've learned my lesson, Mom. I know I should've known better. All right; yeah, I understand…I'll stop by when I can." Katherine pressed the phone to her throbbing temple. She thought her head would explode.

Her mother had terrible luck with relationships, too…but none of them were like Mike, and Katherine had never told her just how bad things were. Her mother simply found the love-them-and-leave-them kind. Katherine couldn't get rid of her ex-husband, no matter how hard she tried.

She wiped at her eyes, set her shoulders, and then clenched her jaw. *Let's get this over with.* The key turned in the ignition and her foot hit the gas before she peeled out onto the road. The drive to the storage facility went quickly. Lulled into a daze, Katherine didn't even see the blur of scenery flashing by. Her thoughts turned to the way the evening had ended so badly the night before.

Suddenly, the inside of her car felt hot and stuffy, making her sweaty. Like a steamy day spent working in a factory, bent over a sewing machine, feeding the material through. Lifting heavy bolts of fabric. Dead on her feet. Being on the lake with Chester for their wedding trip…it would be heaven…Katherine saw Grace sliding beneath the surface of the water and she had to pull over. What was wrong with her? She had to stop reading that book and watching those movies with Charlie.

Her hand trailed to her stomach. She missed that fullness, the slight roundness that had been there when her child was growing inside of her…feeling those little flutters of movement, that conversation inside of her that was ongoing, never-ending between the two of them. She'd been wretched after she lost the baby…truly feeling a misery beyond compare, but suicidal? No, that was one thing that Katherine never wanted to do.

She couldn't believe that Grace wanted to, either. The woman in her dream had reached for Chester's hand, calling out his name. She didn't go willingly to her watery grave. Above all else, there was a desperate will to live that tore Katherine from sleep their first night on Ward's Pond, as stark terror coursed through her veins. No, Grace Brown did not want to die.

Katherine slowed and pulled up at the entrance of SafeKeeping, confused as to how her car found the way to the storage facility. It seemed that the drive began only minutes ago. *Or was it a lifetime ago?* Sometimes, she felt unspeakably old. With her nerves jangling and butterflies kicking up a whirlwind in her stomach, she hurried to her unit. Her breath came out in a rush. Mike wasn't there.

She waited with arms crossed, tapping her foot. Five minutes passed. And then ten. Fifteen. Katherine paced to and fro, wearing a small track in the dirt in front of the metal door. It would figure he was late. *Probably at a bar somewhere or just out of spite.* Ominous clouds gathered overhead. *The hell with him.*

Katherine flung the door open, pulled out the grill, and slammed the door shut. She sealed the lock, jumping when a loud rumble of thunder shook the quiet. Mountainous, brooding storm clouds were getting closer, the wind beginning to pick up and tug at her hair. A grin stretched across her face as she left the pricey gas grill out in the open just as the sky let loose.

Good. Let his baby rust. Maybe it would get ruined—the way Mike ruined her. If she was really lucky, it'd get struck by lightning. Talk about a sizzling experience. Getting drenched, she jogged away as a flash crackled across the sky. Another boom of thunder shook the world, and Michael Graciano jumped out of his truck across the street from her car.

"Katherine, where are you going? What about the grill?" His eyes flashed dangerously; his hands curled into fists. His mouth turned down in a menacing sneer, which was always his favorite thing to wear.

"It's sitting there. Go get it." *Hope it's a shocking experience.* She dashed for her car, her heart batting against her ribs, and she couldn't breathe. Her hand touched the door handle when Mike grabbed her arm hard enough to hurt, his fingers closing like a steel vise.

"Let go! You're hurting me!" She planted her feet and pulled in the opposite direction. She might as well have pulled on a concrete wall.

"We're not through yet, Katherine. You are still mine and I'm not ready to let you go." He stepped in closer. She could smell his breath. It reeked of alcohol, and her heart sank. There was no reasoning with him when he was drunk. Katherine had learned that the hard way.

"That's too bad, Mike, because the restraining order says you have to." His hand tightened around her wrist. She felt like it might snap. "Ow! Stop hurting me! Haven't you already done enough?"

Her voice crept toward a scream and she started to struggle, kicking at his shin, yanking against him, not really caring if he broke her wrist. *Have to get away!* She started hitting him with her purse. He drew her in closer and raised his fist, snarling. "You're my wife, Katherine! *Enough of this!*"

"Hey! What're you doing over there? Leave her alone!" A police officer—probably called by the property manager—approached, hand on his holstered weapon.

Mike only held on even tighter. When she looked up at him, stark terror coursed through her and stole the breath from her lungs. *Til death do us part* echoed in her mind. He wouldn't ever let her go. Never. The murderous glare said more than words ever could. He wanted to kill her. After one hard shake, her head snapped back, her teeth clacking together.

"I said *leave...her...alone* or I will shoot you." The officer's gun was out of the holster and leveled at her soon-to-be ex-husband's chest. For one terrible instant, she actually hoped he'd fire.

Mike's grip loosened enough for her to slip away. Katherine pulled her car door open with trembling hands, shut it, locked it, and then started the engine. The officer gestured for her to stop, but she peeled out. She didn't want to talk to him, didn't want to stop. All Katherine wanted to do was get as far away from Mike as possible.

After twenty minutes of driving through a downpour so heavy it was impossible to see, a shaking and sobbing Katherine pulled into a parking lot. A raging river of pain rushed back in, threatening to drown her. *Like Grace Brown.* Her arms wrapped around her stomach as her body rocked. *I hope he didn't hurt that officer.* Another thought came unbidden. *I hope Chester didn't kill Grace.* Somehow, it mattered to her more than ever to know that Charlie Baxter's distant relative couldn't be guilty of such a heinous crime, but what if he was?

SOPPING WET. ARM THROBBING. HEART ACHING. Katherine managed to find her way back to the welcome haven of Dolgeville, back to her secret corner of the world that Michael Graciano didn't know about—*yet.* A place to lick her wounds, heal, and move on with her life. As she drove down Main Street, Arthur's called to her. She just wanted something to make her forget for a little while. A nice glass of sweet, red wine. Maybe a whiskey sour. Or a strawberry daiquiri. To stay in a place where *nobody* knew her name.

Katherine was waiting at the stoplight when she looked to the left, to the East Canada Creek, and saw a familiar figure standing by the bank. It was a woman in white with dark hair pulled back and twisted in a bun. Her mournful gaze met Katherine's, taking her breath away, making her squeeze her eyes shut. She licked her lips that had gone dry as paper. *Look again.* The apparition...or whatever she was...was now gone. *Yes. A glass of oblivion is definitely in order. Perhaps an entire bottle.*

Katherine found a spot in the lot across the street, keeping her head down on her way into the bar and restaurant. She wasn't in the mood for any more encounters, ghostly or human. All she wanted was a quiet table in the corner of the bar where she could find a slip of solitude.

Someone was singing, "Won't you come home, Bill Bailey?" as the door shut behind her. She had to blink a bit to let her eyes adjust to the dim, smoky atmosphere in the tavern. At the far end of the bar, another all-too-familiar figure sat hunched over a bottle of beer, singing to himself and getting louder, muttering something about Grace's favorite song. She expected his performance would become more boisterous the more drinks he had. Another verse and her stomach pitched. Hearing him sing that song simply tore at her heart. "Charlie?"

He cut himself off and craned his neck to look her way. His white shirt was rolled up to the elbows, as if he'd been working for hours—to the point of becoming decidedly rumpled. His hair was tousled, as if he'd run his fingers through it too many times. His eyes were clouded with drinks and something else—some kind of darkness—although his smile was genuine as he called out, "Well, if it isn't Grace Brown!" His eyes widened, and for an instant, his face cracked, but he covered it with a laugh. "Sorry! The bottle's talking! I mean, Katherine Grace Brown! Hello, beautiful! Sit; please, sit. A drink for the young lady...whatever she likes...and bring me another. Make it a boilermaker with the strongest whiskey you've got."

Charlie smacked some money on the smooth surface of the bar and hopped down from his stool, nearly falling over in the process. He caught himself and pulled out a stool for Katherine, giving her a bow. "Please...sit down." As she obliged, he leaned in and brushed her cheek with a kiss, his fingers running over her hair and down her arm, until they clasped her hand. He held on tightly, staring at her intently, as if reassuring himself that she was real. "*You* are a sight for sore eyes."

"You, too, Charlie." She smiled, but then inexplicable tears came up, seeing him in such a state. Something had upset him. She glanced down at his feet, seeing his briefcase. He'd uncovered something new. Hard to swallow. Unlike the beer, judging by the empty bottles lined up in front of him.

The bartender swapped out Charlie's empty bottle for a tall glass that frothed as he dropped in a shot of whiskey. Glancing at the young man before him with a wince and a shake of his head, he stopped in front of Katherine. "What'll it be, miss?"

"A glass of red wine, please. Something light, sweet." He gave a nod, and the drink was quickly placed in front of her. She sipped it even as Charlie resumed his song, cranking the volume up louder. Someone shouted for him to pick something new, while others grumbled in agreement. *How long has he been singing that song? How long has he been in this bar?* Katherine took another sip of her drink and set her hand on his arm. "Charlie, listen to me. It's time to go home."

She laid money down on the bar to make sure the tab was covered and then stepped down. Laughing, he slid off his stool and began to sway, his legs nearly giving out beneath him. Katherine slung his arm over her shoulder and headed for the exit.

"Wait! My bag!" Eyes dark, mouth turning down, he whipped around and stumbled his way back to his chair, taking up his briefcase. He knocked into another man in the bar, sloshing the guy's drink all over the place. The customer glowered and went to shove him, but Charlie raised his hand. "Sorry. So sorry. I'm pitifully drunk. I'll pay for that." He dropped the briefcase and fished in his pocket, pulling out a ten-dollar bill. "That ought to be more than 'nough. Buy 'nother on me."

"Please excuse us." Katherine picked up his bag and ducked under Charlie's arm once again. She staggered under his weight as they wove their way to her car. Opening the passenger door, she helped him in and clicked his seat belt. "Safety first," she whispered, setting his briefcase in the back seat before walking around to her side and starting the car.

A dull headache throbbed at the base of her skull, promising to be a future humdinger. *Should have stayed in bed today.*

As they rolled to a stop in the parking area at Ward's Pond, the sun was touching down on the horizon, a burning ball of fire sinking into the surface of the pond. Charlie stared at it until his eyes began to water. He swiped his sleeve across his face and turned to Katherine, taking her hand. He was dead serious and practically sober already. "I'm sorry, Katherine. I...I don't usually drink like this. I just had a rough day."

"Me too." She kissed his cheek in sympathy and helped Charlie to his room, slipping off his shoes. Katherine pulled back the covers and let him lie down before covering him up. He smiled at her and started to hum the same song again. *At least he's a nice drunk.* She rested her hands on his chest. "Get some sleep, Charlie. Like my Nana says, things are bound to look better in the morning."

Katherine then went to her own room, pulled off her clothes, and slipped into her nightgown. She intended to take her own advice. As she closed her eyes, the dam finally broke, her tears flowing like a river. She buried her face in her pillow to cover the sound of her weeping. Far in the back of her mind, a line of a song from childhood drifted through. *The sun will come out tomorrow...*

She certainly hoped so. Since right now, all Katherine could see were clouds.

7

"WE MEET AGAIN." CHARLIE WINCED AT THE SOUND OF HIS OWN VOICE as he greeted Katherine at breakfast. How many beers had he drunk? He choked down a few aspirin and pressed the cold glass of orange juice to his forehead. "I'm nursing a granddaddy of a hangover. I apologize for anything inappropriate I might've done or said last night. I don't do this too often, and I don't remember much."

Katherine patted his hand. "You were fine, really. You're a friendly drunk, although I'm glad it's not the norm because I'm not strong enough to carry you." She dipped her head and stirred her tea. When she picked it up, her hands trembled slightly, some of the hot brew sloshing over the side.

Charlie forgot about his own worries long enough to notice that the woman beside him looked drawn, her eyes sad—as if her light had been snuffed out. He took her hand in both of his, forcing her to meet his eye. "You okay? Listen, I'll do a better job picking a light bedtime movie next time—you know, something like *When Harry Met Sally*. Something funny. Romantic, even. No doom and gloom. No death. I'm really sorry. Should've known better than to show you *A Place in the Sun*."

She gave him a ghost of a smile. "No. That was fine. I owe you an apology for being so miserable when I left. I had a text from my ex-husband and knew I'd have to hash it out with him. I've tried ignoring him in the past, and it only makes things worse. Talk about texting harassment. He really knows how to blow up a phone. It turns out I had to meet him at my storage unit. He wanted his beloved grill. I think Mike loved that appliance more than me."

Her sleeve slid as she picked up her cup again, revealing a nasty bruise around her wrist. Charlie's body went rigid, his breath coming out in a rush. It looked like the imprint of large fingers wrapped around her slender arm. He set his hand lightly on her shoulder. "Katherine…what…Mike had something to do with *this*?"

Her eyes filled with tears and she pulled her arm away, tugging her sleeve down to cover the marks on her fair skin. "I don't want to talk about it. Let's just say it's a part of why I wanted a divorce."

You should have been with her instead of buried in a library with old news. Chester and Grace are gone. Katherine's here. For now. His appetite disappeared. Charlie finished his cup of coffee and considered taking an entire bottle of aspirin to hopefully relieve the pounding in his head. Yet somehow, he suspected thrashing Mike Graciano was the only remedy.

"Listen, you wanna go for a drive with me? We can just hang out for a while. No research. No divorce stuff. Have some badly needed downtime. What do you say?"

She tucked a strand of her hair behind her ear. "That'd be nice. Mike never—"

"Mike never what?" He waited patiently for the crack in her protective shield to widen, to let him in.

"My ex-husband never wanted to go for a drive or do anything I wanted to do." Katherine stared down at her plate as her fork pushed the food around without actually letting her eat any of it.

Charlie set his hand beneath her chin and pressed up gently until she looked at him. "I'd say it's high time you went for a drive."

THEY WENDED THEIR WAY THROUGH THE ADIRONDACKS FOR HOURS, just driving with no destination in mind. He made sure to steer clear of any place near the path Chester and Grace followed. His old GTO didn't get close to the vicinity of Katherine's life with Mike Graciano. They stopped at a hot dog stand, a beach at one of the small lakes, any gift shops they could find, and an ice cream stand. As they climbed in for their return trip in Black Beauty—as he'd dubbed the family heirloom passed on from his father—Katherine stroked the dashboard, eyes lit up in appreciation. "This is one fine ride. If I owned this car, I'd take it anywhere I pleased."

Charlie slid her a grin. "Sign me up. I'll be your driver." *And anything else you want me to be.*

The sun was on its downward slope in the sky as they chugged along toward Caroga Lake, taking a roundabout way to get back to Dolgeville. The radio was playing something lazy from the fifties. Katherine laid her head on Charlie's shoulder. "Careful. We might even see a sasquatch, Chester." Her voice was sleepy, her eyes dreamy...

Charlie jerked the car to the shoulder, slamming on the brakes, coming to a squealing halt. The rumble of the motor continued to hum as his breath came hard and fast, as if he'd been running a marathon. His hands gripped the wheel so tightly, he thought it would be easy to pull the thing right off the dashboard. Finally, he calmed enough to assemble words. "Whatever has been going on with you, me, this story, all of this...let's get one thing straight. *I'm not Chester.*"

Katherine laid her hand on his arm. His muscles were so tense that they'd begun to spasm painfully. He ignored them. "I'm sorry, Charlie, but *I* want to make something clear to *you*. I'm not Grace."

Tentatively, she laid her palm on his cheek. He could feel a slight quiver running through her. Slowly, Charlie turned to face her, his forehead dropping until it was propped against hers. He nearly choked up as he whispered, "How about we just be you and me? No baggage. No past. Only the present...and maybe a future?" Her smile held for an instant before her face crumpled and she rested her head against his chest. His shirt was soon damp from tears. A few might have even been his own.

THE WATER SWISHED AGAINST THE DOCK OFF OF SHERMAN'S, an old amusement park on the shore of Caroga Lake that had been closed for years. For an instant, Charlie had the unsettling feeling of being in a boat. His thoughts turned to Chester and Grace yet again. He yanked his mind off that beaten path and focused on the woman at his side. "Do you really believe in Sasquatch?"

She laughed and threaded her fingers through his. "Oh, absolutely. Aliens, vampires, fairies, God and His angels. All of it. After all, what do I have to lose to think I share this world with some amazing creatures unlike anything else on the planet? I think we'd be pretty conceited to think we're the only thing out there. As for the monsters, sometimes I don't think there's anything nastier than a human being." A tremor ran through her, and she bit down on her lip. What kind of demon was Katherine facing? He had a feeling that it walked around in a man by the name of Mike Graciano.

Charlie closed his eyes. Otherwise, she'd see how much he was hurting. Katherine had enough on her plate. "I wish that's what I was writing about, Bigfoot or UFOs—something that doesn't seem real to me." His words trailed off as the familiar ache clutched at his heart. If he sat up and looked hard, Chester would be there, no doubt about it.

Katherine squeezed his hand. "You didn't have a choice. This story chose you."

He sat up fast, cupping his face in his hands. "That's the problem. It's got a death grip on me. Chester and Grace? Those two are so real they break my heart. No matter what really happened, whether Grace tripped and fell, committed suicide, or Chester killed her, there's one undeniable truth. He didn't do right by her. Either he didn't try to save her, or he was too much of a coward to tell everyone what happened to her. He just let her die in that lake."

Katherine turned to rest a palm on his cheek. Her touch was cool and soothing. "You don't know what happened that night. *None* of us know. Chester might have tried but *couldn't* save her. Maybe that's why you've been drawn to this story—to make sure the truth is told. For your sake. For Grace."

Charlie studied her closely. His voice was hoarse when he spoke. "Why have *you* been pulled into this mess?"

"To make sure you follow your heart and don't give up." She laid her hand on his chest, over the steady beating that sounded in his ears. "It's a good heart. The kind that will stand by a person to the end and see things through."

Impulsively, Charlie gathered Katherine up and settled her on his lap. "I *will* see it through. I promise. I'm in too deep to give up now."

She reached up to kiss him, her hands hooking around his neck. "I'll be by your side." Charlie gave himself to the kiss. In that instant, he didn't care if they never left the dock.

KATHERINE'S FEET CARRIED HER ACROSS THE EXTENSIVE LAWN at Ward's Pond, her mind too busy and full to let her stand still. She rubbed at her arms, wondering how long her life would be on hold. When would the waiting game end? She was desperately waiting for the divorce papers to be signed. And waiting to move forward in her life, while also waiting to forget about the past and think about the future. Or to refrain from looking over her shoulder for Mike.

A chill ran through her, as it always did, every time that man crossed her mind. She sat down by the pond and tried to find comfort in the family of geese following each other from one side to the other. Seeing the babies all in a row behind their mother made her smile...until the date hit her. Like a sucker punch in the gut, making the pain settle in the pit of her stomach. *Today.* Today marked the date that her world was irrevocably changed by a loss so deep and so hurtful, she'd never fully recover. She buried her face in her hands, letting the sobs come. Katherine had cried many tears. The well should've run dry, but still they came, and the crack in her heart split open even wider.

CHARLIE'S EYES BLURRED. HIS HEAD ACHED FROM READING FOR HOURS ON END and the lack of sleep drove him crazy. He eyed the bed and considered lying down for a while. Thankfully, Chester had left him alone for the past few days. Maybe the ghost's work was done after the trip to the library. Without his visitor, sleep might actually come for him.

Charlie stood up and reached his arms over his head, stretching until his back cracked. He winced. *You are way too young to sound like that.* He walked over to the window, planning to close the curtains, when a figure by the pond made him freeze. His hand pressed against the glass. *Grace!*

A woman in white, her hair done up in some type of a twist at the back of her head, sat by the water. *Great. I'm swapping one ghost for another.* He cursed and shook his head, then looked again and let out a sigh of relief. It was Katherine, and she looked unspeakably lovely—yet there was something about her that was so lonely, the way she was hunched over with her face in her hands.

Intent on giving her whatever he had to give, he straightened his shirt and slipped into his shoes. A sweep of the comb through his hair made some order out of the mess. He tended to run his hands through the heavy strands as he worked. He hurried down the stairs, taking them two at a time, and grabbed a handful of daisies on the way. Something sweet and innocent, like Katherine.

Tell Grace. Charlie nearly dropped his wild bouquet. His ghostly visitor had returned and stood beside Katherine's bench; his hand extended toward her. Charlie's jaw clenched. *She's not Grace. Leave her alone.* In a blink, Chester was gone.

Charlie sat down beside Katherine and nudged her arm. She sat up, wiping tears off her face quickly as he handed her the flowers. "Just a little something. You look like you need cheering up."

She buried her face in them. "They're lovely. I've always loved daisies. I was going to name my little girl Daisy..." The words stopped abruptly as Katherine clamped her mouth shut, but the tears, never far from the surface, spilled down her face.

Charlie threaded his fingers through hers. "What happened to your little girl, Katherine?"

She wrapped an arm around her stomach, as if trying to protect something that was already gone. "She...she didn't make it. I lost her...five months into my pregnancy. Today's the anniversary of her death. I would have called her Daisy Mae."

"I'm so sorry." Charlie didn't—couldn't—say any more. He wrapped an arm around her and cradled her against his chest, letting Katherine cry herself out. All the while, he couldn't help but think about Grace Mae Brown, who fell in love with the wrong guy over a hundred years ago. Had Katherine followed the same path? His arm tightened around her. One thing was certain, though. He wouldn't let Mike Graciano get near her. *If only someone had stopped Chester,* his inner voice nagged. *Right...but no one made Grace go out with him in the first place, even though they both knew it was wrong. The attraction of the forbidden...and they'd paid the price...and so had their unborn child.*

The weeping willows reached down toward the water, swaying with the breeze, as if in mourning. Holding the young woman beside him, Charlie ached for her. For Grace. A gentle rain began to fall as the world cried for them.

8

KATHERINE SAT IN FRONT OF HER VANITY, STARING INTO THE MIRROR, brushing her hair because it soothed her. She closed her eyes and then fell into the rhythm, until something made her open them. The figure of a small woman stood behind her, dressed in white. Her hair was pulled up into the style of a Gibson girl while her large, dark eyes gazed at Katherine as if they could see right through her. She didn't do anything. Didn't say anything. Simply stood there as a deafening silence fell over the room. The only thing Katherine could hear was a thrumming in her ears in time with the hammering in her chest.

Her heart stuttered. She squeezed her eyes shut, took a deep breath, and whipped around to…nothing—except a fluttering curtain. Rubbing at her arms, suddenly chilled to the bone, she stood up, crossed the room, and closed the window. She locked it with a quick snap of her wrist. She would *not* be reading any more of that *Murder in the Adirondacks* anytime soon. It was really making her imagination run away with her.

Katherine resisted the temptation to cross the hall and knock on Charlie's door. He *had* told her to stay away from that book. She stuffed it in her drawer beneath some clothes, undressed herself, and slid into bed. It might have been childish, but she left a light on.

WAKE UP! AN URGENT VOICE SPOKE IN HIS HEAD. The voice was oddly familiar, like an old friend. Charlie sat up abruptly to see a ghostly figure by the side of his bed, opaque and dressed in a suit. His dark hair was slicked back away from his face, his shadowy eyes brooding. "Chester?!"

The man raised his hand and pointed to the window. Charlie dashed across the room, looking out to see a woman in white walking barefoot across the grass in nothing but a cotton nightgown, her hair forming a darkened curtain down her back. The wind tugged at the heavy strands, whipping them in a wild tangle around her. This was no ghost.

"Katherine!" he shouted but could not be heard from the open window.

Panic rising, Charlie shrugged into his bathrobe and stepped into his slippers. He ran down the stairs and out onto the porch, frozen by the scene that unfolded before him. Katherine had reached the pond, and inexplicably, there was a rowboat out in the middle. But he could see through it to the other side of the pond. A woman sat at one end, a man at the other. Squinting at the apparition, he could see that the man was one and the same as the ghostly visitor in his room. Before Charlie had any time to think about the insanity of seeing a haunted boat that did not belong on Ward's Pond, the woman in the middle of the pond stood up.

"No!" His shout rose up, but she didn't hear him. It was like shouting at a movie while the film was still rolling, knowing what was coming with no way to change the outcome. In a flash, she lost her balance and toppled overboard. The man—*Chester! By God, it's Chester!*—stood and reached for her, catching her fingers for an instant, but she slipped out of his hands and the boat overturned.

"Chester, help me!" A woman's tormented scream jolted him into motion. Charlie glanced to the shore, watching in horror as Katherine walked straight into the pond toward the ghost boat.

Charlie sprinted across the lawn, shedding his slippers, robe, and pajama top, shimmying down to his underwear last and leaving a trail of clothes behind him. With a glance at Katherine, he strode forward and bellowed with everything he had, "Katherine, *STOP!*" She continued on, oblivious. Exactly how deep was the water?

Charlie reached the shore; on the opposite side, he saw Chester once again, reaching toward Katherine imploringly…and then the boat vanished. Charlie dove into the pond without hesitation as Katherine took one more step. She hit a drop, going in up to her chin, her arms flailing wildly. *What if she can't swim?* Inspiration struck and he called out, "Grace, stop!"

She became still and her eyes opened wide, then rolled back into her head. Katherine went under, one white hand reaching toward the moon. Charlie's gut twisted so hard he almost got sick. Thankful he'd been on the swim team in high school, his body remembered what to do, taking powerful strokes toward the middle of the pond.

Even though it was May, the water was still cold. The air temperature had dropped below 50 degrees at night. The water felt like it was nearly freezing. Charlie's insides hurt, and his entire body was getting heavier. One more desperate lunge, and he grabbed Katherine's hand just as she went under. *Like Grace.*

With his heart beating hard enough to burst, Charlie hooked an arm around Katherine's neck and started back to shore. Shaking, he dragged her out onto the grass and knelt beside her. She wasn't breathing; her pale skin felt as cold as marble. She was a ghastly white in the light of the moon, her dark hair pasted to her cheek. Charlie shook her hard even as his body started to quiver uncontrollably with the chill, his teeth chattering.

"Katherine, come back to me! Come back, God help me…" He bowed his head, pressing his ear to her chest. A great gasp rose up and she started to cough, turning her head to the side as water came up, running onto the grass. Her chest rose and fell as she drew deep breaths. Charlie nearly broke down with relief.

He stood on wobbly legs and scurried across the lawn to collect his clothes. Not wishing to scandalize Eva or her neighbors, he quickly pulled on his pajamas. Charlie grabbed his robe and wrapped it around Katherine. He scooped up his slippers, not willing to waste any more time, and jogged across the lawn. Then he hurried her through the doorway and up the stairs, right to her room. He turned the shower on high and carried her into the bathroom.

"Do you need my help?" he asked her quietly. She stared at him for a moment, her mind slowly processing his words after such a scare. "Katherine? Want me to get Eva or call a doctor?"

She shook her head, gazing around her bathroom as if she didn't know how they'd managed to get there. Maybe she didn't. "No, no. I'm fine. I'll be out in a few minutes. Thank you."

When she walked out of the bathroom in another white nightgown that Charlie found and set on the sink, a cloud of steam came with her. Her dark hair was pulled away from her face and for one awful moment, she looked like Grace. Charlie took a step toward her and she raced into his solid arms. She started to cry the instant his warmth closed around her. "I don't know what happened! I can't remember! One moment I was in bed, the next…I was in the pond! Am I going crazy, Charlie?"

"No, not at all. You're not crazy, Katherine. Some strange things have been happening to the both of us. But I don't want you to worry about that right now. You need to lie down, get warm, and then get some sleep. We'll figure this out tomorrow." She nodded and went quietly, lying down and allowing him to cover her up with her quilt.

Charlie kissed her good night on the crown of her head and curled up in the large, soft chair by the side of her bed. He wrapped up in a blanket, shivering all night long. Every time he closed his eyes, he saw the scene on the pond play out again. When the darkness began to fade into a light gray, he felt her hand on his—warm while his was still like ice. She sat on his lap and pulled her blanket around them both, turning into his human heater.

"You saved my life." She pressed her lips to his, sending a rush of welcome heat through his veins.

"I'd do it again. Every day of the week." His lips pressed to hers and the flames of her touch engulfed him, banishing the fear and ice that had nearly stopped his heart.

Katherine burrowed in closer to him. She was trembling. Charlie had to ask. "Do you remember what you dreamed, what led you to the pond?"

"It…it was Chester…and Grace…in the boat—like the dream I had the first night."

His breath caught. He ran his hand over her hair, his fingers shaking. "That's what you dreamed the night we met? You saw Grace's death?"

She looked up at him, her eyes wide with fright. "I *was* Grace," she whispered.

His heart twisted and he bit down on his lip. "I'm sorry you've been brought into this, Katherine. So sorry."

She caught a tear sliding down his cheek, resting her palm on his face. "I guess we're meant to be a safe harbor for each other until you find the truth." As he held her close, feeling her shaking, Charlie couldn't help but wonder. *Has Katherine been looking for a safe harbor at Ward's Pond from the very beginning? What shark is out there trying to snap her in its jaws?*

CHARLIE COULDN'T FALL BACK ASLEEP, unable to stop thinking about Katherine's dreams and her frightful experience at the pond. He *had* to find out what really happened, beyond the bald facts of the case. Charlie waited until he knew Katherine was in a deep sleep, her breathing steady as he watched the sun come tiptoeing in. Her room was transformed into a cheerful place—not the stuff of nightmares and horror movies—as the glow of golden rays made the highlights in her hair shimmer.

Charlie stroked a strand of her hair. Her mouth curled up in a hint of a smile, but she didn't wake. She still looked pale…and that bothered him to no end. He carefully laid her back in her bed, still wrapped in a cocoon of blankets, and padded on bare feet out of the room, scooping up his slippers on the way out.

He stood under a pounding shower for a long time, trying to erase his memories from the middle of the night, but the images were too deeply ingrained to let go of him. Charlie dressed quickly and then went down to the dining room for a cup of coffee. His stomach couldn't take anything else. He carried his mug out to the porch and sat down, staring out at the pond. His insides were simmering, like a powder keg ready to explode.

Why? Why were Chester and Grace hanging around the bed and breakfast? This place wasn't a part of their fateful "wedding" journey. Charlie had done his homework. Chester had taken Grace several places, including DeRuyter, Utica, and Old Forge, before ending up at the Glenmore Hotel on Big Moose Lake. He'd called himself Carl Grahm from Albany to use a cover name that would match the initials on his suitcase. Never had there been any reference of a stop in Dolgeville or at Ward's Pond.

Charlie took another sip of his coffee, trying to pierce through the fog of fatigue and confusion weighing down on his mind when a thought hit him like a lightning bolt. *It's not the place. It's YOU.* He was the connection, the focal point drawing their ghosts' attention as he sifted through the past. Charlie sank back in his chair and pressed a hand to his eyes. He was the accused's relative. Staying at the home of the man who sent Chester to the electric chair while he rooted around in the past probably tipped the scales in the spiritual world. What had Charlie done? Had he opened some kind of door and let them in? Somehow, he had to make this right. *For everyone.*

With his stomach churning too much to take any more, he pitched his coffee over the railing and went back inside. Food was still laid out on the dining room table. He made a plate for Katherine, placed it on a tray with fixings for hot tea, and then brought it up to her room. She still slept, the bloom of color slowly returning to her cheeks. Charlie set the tray on her dresser and returned to his room.

Back to the trenches. There had to be something he was missing. He pulled out his notes about the timeline between Chester and Grace, from their meeting in 1905 to their ongoing relationship, her pregnancy, and their trip in July of 1906. Grace's chest contained all her clothes. She definitely expected a long trip, yet Chester had only one suitcase with his own initials. He'd used a cover name, but that would be expected for an unmarried couple. They wouldn't have wanted to make anyone suspicious. The fact that Chester packed light suggested he'd not be going away with Grace. It supported the theory that they were on their way to a home for unwed mothers. If Chester had all the details worked out, from a cover name to a place for Grace to stay and a way back to his old life, why would he take her out on Big Moose Lake to kill her? Why bring a tennis racket? Chester and Grace would *not* have been playing tennis, nor would it make any sense to bring one on the boat. Charlie was convinced. There *were* holes in the prosecution's case…

He stared at his computer screen, wanting nothing more than to throw the blasted thing out the window, when an article popped up about Chester's prison journal. It had been in safekeeping with the Gillette family since his death—passed down by his sister, Hazel—the one person who continued to stay in touch while he was in prison. His grandniece, Marylynn McWade-Murray, donated the journal to the Hamilton College. Perhaps Chester's own words in his final days as he awaited his execution would reveal something that the others had missed.

A compilation of the journal entries, as well as Chester's final letters to his sister and a female friend, had been published by Jack Sherman and Craig Brandon soon after the original artifact had been unearthed from the family collection. Charlie had a copy sitting in his briefcase. How much easier would his life be if he simply thumbed through that publication? Yet something kept poking at him, like a splinter buried deep. Festering. Throbbing. He had to hold the original journal of his ancestor's last words *in his own hands*.

Charlie looked up the college on his phone and dialed before he lost his nerve. An appointment was set with the head librarian. In a few days, he'd capture a piece of his family's past and possibly find the proverbial needle in the haystack.

Unsettled and on edge, he dove back into his typing, flying through the chapters of his book as his writing continued to take shape. The hours wore on and his fingers began to cramp up, the words like slippery fish that he could no longer catch to put down on the page. With his head pounding too hard to see straight anymore, Charlie stretched out on his bed. The moment he closed his eyes, the voice that had been haunting him for days spoke in his head. *Grace. Tell Grace.* Charlie spent another fretful night with Chester's shadow hovering on the edge of his mind.

KATHERINE CAME DOWN TO BREAKFAST THE NEXT MORNING, STILL SHAKEN FROM HER DREAM. She laughed nervously, taking a restorative sip of tea. "Can't believe I slept all day yesterday. I guess I was really tired. I've never been a sleepwalker before. It's exhausting."

Eva slipped in with her regular breakfast request of toast, yogurt, and tea. Charlie watched Katherine fiddle with her food even as he pushed his eggs around on his plate. *His* appetite had disappeared. "I just can't stop thinking about that nightmare. It felt like I was Grace...like before...on my first night here."

Charlie straightened as a thought occurred to him, one he'd buried the night they first met. He rested his hand on the nape of Katherine's neck and then gently massaged muscles that had gone tight. "Ever think that you might be connected to Grace? Your name might not be a coincidence. I could do some research for you, rule it out."

She shot to her feet; her face tight. Her hands were balled into fists, perhaps to keep from shaking. "No, I *don't* want to find out. Whatever brought me here, that's enough. Haven't you ever thought some bones should stay buried, Charlie?" Not giving him a chance to answer, she hurried out of the room.

Charlie set his coffee down fast and raked a hand through his hair. Why did his mother have to ask him to write *this* story? It was one that entangled him so deeply, he didn't think he'd ever untie the knots. Worse, the Gillette-Brown murder had Katherine wrapped up just as tightly. He had half a mind to try a genealogy search, to follow the trail, to find out if she *was* actually related to Grace Mae Brown.

Something felt wrong about it, too intrusive. *Admit it. This is one secret that you don't want to know about, because if she IS a distant relative, are the two of you destined to play out history all over again?* A shudder ran through him as he thought of that terrifying moment she'd gone into the pond, and his fist slammed down on the table, making the silverware and china jump. "No! *I'll be damned, no.* I'll make it right!" Charlie muttered his solemn vow and left the table, taking up his briefcase and his keys, quietly thanking Eva on the way out.

A map sat in his glove compartment, one he'd marked off when the journey into his family's past began, following the path on the fateful final voyage of Chester Gillette and Grace Brown. A trip that began in DeRuyter, moving on to Utica, then on to Tupper Lake, Old Forge, and ending in Big Moose Lake—for Grace. Charlie set his GPS and retraced their travels, his frustration mounting with every stop. Still no answers, no leads. Nothing but old news. As he arrived in Old Forge, a downpour hit, buffeting his car with hail and horrendous winds. By the time the weather finally let up, darkness had fallen. Big Moose Lake and Inlet, the end of the line for Chester, would have to wait.

Charlie's mind turned to Katherine, worry for her nagging at him. As he prepared to pull away from the Goodsell Museum, as fitting a place as any to wait out nature's fury, Chester appeared outside his driver's-side window. Thunder rolled off in the distance and lightning continued to crackle across the sky as that all-too-familiar voice whispered in his mind. *Tell Grace.*

"What do you want from me, Chester?!" A big boom shook the night as a tree snapped only a few feet behind Charlie's car. When he looked out his window, his ghostly companion was gone. With a heavy heart and a gaping pit in his stomach that was growing by the day, he turned the car toward home. Whatever he was supposed to tell Grace remained a mystery. He didn't know what to tell Katherine, either.

9

KATHERINE SAT ON THE PORCH, IN AWE OF NATURE'S LIGHT SHOW. Thunder rumbled all around her as the lights flashed in a panorama across the sky. The weather, in all its glory, made its power known—yet she wasn't afraid. Growing up, she always used to sit on Mama's or Nana's lap, on the porch or at the window, watching what God did best. If only she could face Mike Graciano with no fear.

Footsteps sounded on the stairs and she prepared to flee, the terror never far from the surface that her soon-to-be ex-husband would come and take her. And she'd be kicking and screaming all the way. A rush of relief made her light-headed as Charlie reached the top step, until she took a closer look and her jaw dropped. He was soaking wet, shaking so hard his teeth were chattering. Even though it was late June and warm, the temperature had dropped considerably with the storm.

Katherine hopped up from her perch. "Goodness, Charlie! You'll catch your death. Come inside and I'll help you get dried off and warmed up." She grabbed his arm. He was so tense; the man could have been made out of stone.

Katherine opened the door and led him inside. "Wait here a moment," she instructed at the bottom of the steps, wincing at the puddle that was already forming by his feet. She hurried down the hall and knocked on Eva's private quarters. The lively young woman poked her head of wild, dark curls out the door. "Eva, could you please bring up some coffee and tea? Charlie looks like a drowned rat. He got caught in the storm." Their hostess willingly agreed.

Katherine returned to Charlie's side to find him swaying where he stood, trembling even more. She took his arm and led him up the stairs to his room in an ironically reverse move of what he had done for her after she inexplicably walked into the pond in the middle of the night.

Pushing those memories aside, Katherine poked around until she found his pajamas. She turned on a hot, steamy shower and pointed at the tub. "Get in there to get rid of that chill." To soften her sharp tongue, she rose up and kissed him. His lips were like ice, yet still they burned. She shut the bathroom door behind her and leaned against it, a hand pressed to her heart. Katherine didn't know how much more of the man she could take.

A knock sounded on the door, making her jump. "It's only little ol' me," Eva called out.

Katherine opened it and Eva then bustled in, setting the tray on the dresser. "There you go, dearie. I brought you some brownies, too, just out of the oven. Thought you both would enjoy warming up…although it seems like it's plenty warm between you two!" That set her to laughing as she fanned her face and backed out.

Katherine prepared herself a cup of tea and sat by the window overlooking the pond. She tried to drink the hot brew, but her hands were quivering so badly she had to put it down. She wrapped her arms tightly around herself, struggling to resist temptation. To walk in that bathroom. Envelop herself in steam. Strip out of her clothes and step into that shower with Charlie. Take away those shadows in his eyes, soothe whatever was troubling him—for she had no doubt Charlie's personal storm was much worse than anything Mother Nature had cooked up that night.

The sound of the water beating on the tile made her blood begin to sing, and her heart picked up its pace. She pictured those troubled blue eyes, the fall of chestnut hair that always got in his way, those broad shoulders. As for the rest of the package, her imagination filled in the blanks quite nicely. The heat rushed all the way to her ears, and she closed her eyes, trying to rein in her mind. *Remember. You're on a mission of mercy.*

"Katherine?" Charlie stepped out of the bathroom in striped pajama bottoms that hung low on his hips and a loose blue T-shirt that brought out the color of his eyes, making them all the more powerful. "Are you all right?"

He stepped toward her and laid his hand on her shoulder. She started, like a bolt of electricity shot through her, and stood up fast. Too fast. When would the touch of a man ever stop startling her? *Damn you, Michael Graciano!*

"I'm fine, fine! Eva brought coffee and brownies. I thought you'd like something hot." *Like you.* Mortified, Katherine slammed the door on her racy train of thought and went to the dresser. Somehow, she managed to bring him coffee and a sweet treat without mishap.

He continued to watch her intently, his eyes nearly the color of slate, a sure indicator of the turmoil stirring beneath the surface. "No more strange dreams? No more walks into the pond?" A ripple ran through him as he clenched his jaw: fear. Charlie knew it well, perhaps more so than her. He had to watch her go into that water…and pull her out. *She* slept through the worst of it.

Katherine flipped her hand in the air in dismissal. She didn't want to revisit that night…or that dream. "No, nothing at all. Today was blissfully normal. I was sinfully lazy around here. What did *you* do all day?"

Charlie thanked her and sat down on the edge of the bed. He sipped at his coffee, a line forming between his eyes at the bitter taste. The brownie remained on the plate, untouched. She suspected there was nothing wrong with the food. The problem came from within. "Not much, really. More dead ends."

He quietly told her about his drive without divulging any details. Whether he wanted to spare her heartache or boredom was unclear. "I couldn't stomach finishing it in Big Moose Lake. *That* trip will have to wait for another day."

Or never. Katherine couldn't hold back a shiver, thinking about how hard it must be to research such a morbid case. How did anyone do it, especially those who were connected to the story in some way like Charlie? She took his cup and plate, setting them on the tray. After a few steps back to the bed, she placed her hands firmly on his chest. A shudder ran through her, anxiety never far from the surface, but she beat it down. Mike's shadow would *not* darken this night or this man who needed *her* right now.

"Why don't we finish this evening in a pleasant way? No ghosts. No murders. No research or stories about my ex. Just you…and me." She bent her head and set her lips on his. The effect was electric as his arms came up to wrap around her and pulled her down beside him. A groan rumbled deep inside of him as Charlie pressed his body against hers.

He rose up on his arms, bracing himself as he stared down at her…and she waited for him to make the next move. His face crumpled. "I can't…I can't give you more right now, Katherine. It wouldn't be right. I feel like I'm taking advantage of you and I'm afraid—so damned afraid—that I'll hurt you, that somehow, I've dragged you into this mess. This case has got me turned inside out."

She gently set her finger on his lip. "You could *never* hurt me, and you didn't make any of these strange things happen here on Ward's Pond. For reasons that we can't understand, they just happened. Right now, I don't want to think about what it all means. I just want your company. That's more than enough."

Katherine shifted so that he could slide in under the covers next to her. She pulled up the blankets around them, creating a warm, safe bubble that shut them off from the rest of the world. She pictured Dorothy from *The Wizard of Oz*, clicking her heels together. *There's no place like home.*

But wasn't home more a state of mind or the person that made you feel like you were safe, that you belonged? Could she cast the same spell on this place tonight, with this man, where nothing could hurt either one of them? Katherine had to try.

She gathered the blanket around them and ran her fingers through his hair, stroking until his eyes drooped shut. The line marring his forehead, the crease that had been there since the night she met him, disappeared. His whole body went slack, and his breath came out in a rush. "Prince Charming sleeps," Katherine whispered.

She laid her head against his chest and tumbled over the edge of consciousness next. To slip into sweet dreams. Wrapped in his arms. Entangled in his sheets. Snared in his eyes. His lips sealed against hers as they shared the same air. She woke up to the morning sunlight streaming through open curtains—and his smile, his eyes bright, unclouded by sorrow, fatigue, or frustration.

"Good morning." His voice was low and husky, doing something strange to her insides. It was completely different from the jitters her husband sent through her every time he spoke. Or touched her.

"It is here with you." She tilted her head and he kissed her, eclipsing the sun and every other light in the heavens. The man beside her left no room for Chester, Grace…or Mike Graciano.

CHESTER'S JOURNAL. THE DAY HAD ARRIVED TO COME FACE-TO-FACE with the final writings of the man who had come before him and shared his blood, the subject of so much controversy and the most in-depth research of Charlie's life. As a writer, he understood how personal a journal was. It held one's innermost thoughts. A piece of the soul. And that's why he'd avoided it—until now.

There was no more putting it off. The anniversary of Grace's death was only days away, filling him with a sense of urgency that wouldn't let him rest. To make matters worse, Chester had burdened him with the obligation to carry some sort of message to the deceased woman. Charlie still had no idea what the message was or how he'd possibly deliver it. Go to Big Moose? Travel to her grave site? Sitting in his car in front of the Hamilton College library, he gripped the wheel so tightly, he was sure it would break. He took a deep breath and opened the car door. *Take it one step at a time.*

His feet dragged going up the steps. Through the door. Down the hall. To the office of Marvin Truman, head librarian. Charlie hesitated with his hand on the knob. This was too final, the last piece of the puzzle, but it was something he had to do. It was fitting for today, of all days, when Katherine had trekked off to Syracuse to finalize her divorce. They were both seeking closure. Today, Charlie would close the final chapter on Chester Gillette's life when he looked at the final entry of his journal. They were the last words his ancestor would ever write—or, in essence, say.

The door opened before he had a chance to knock, an older, gray-haired man in a dark suit stepping back in surprise. "Oh, you must be Charlie Baxter, right? I've seen your picture online. Do come in. I'm Marvin." He extended his hand in greeting.

Charlie accepted his handshake and then stepped into a comfortable but not boastful room in rich hues of brown and green. *Like the woodlands.* He imagined the atmosphere was intended to put one at ease, but the glass case on the table with a book sitting inside made his body go rigid. He planted his feet, staring at it, his jaw clenched.

Marvin pressed a hand on his shoulder. "I imagine that this must be very difficult for you, Mr. Baxter. Take your time. I'm in no rush. When you're ready, I will lift the glass and give you white gloves to handle this delicate artifact. I'm sure you realize that it is quite fragile, and you will have to take great care with it. You won't be at liberty to read the actual journal in its entirety, but I do have copies that were made when it first arrived. I've made another set for you that you are free to take with you."

"Thank you. Please. Call me Charlie," he said faintly, as if from far away. His throat was dry, his heart fluttering madly in his chest. The room suddenly felt cold as a breeze passed by him, lifting his hair and making his shirt ripple. The windows were closed and there was no fan in sight.

Charlie gazed at a table on the other side of the room. A dark-haired man stood with his head bowed, his hands resting on the solid oak…a man who had become like a friend — or his conscience. *Chester*. His mind called out.

The figure raised his head and stared him down. *Grace. Tell Grace.* One step forward with his hand raised imploringly, and he was gone.

"That's odd. I just felt a draft in here, but I can't imagine where it would come from." Marvin's pale-green eyes were kind as he nodded to the journal. "Think you're ready now, Charlie?"

Charlie cleared his throat and approached the table. He slipped the gloves on, trying to hide the trembling of his hands while the librarian lifted the glass, putting on a pair of gloves as well. Marvin slowly picked up the book with the greatest care…and turned to the last section. He set the journal in Charlie's hands. Such a small volume to sum up a life. Charlie tilted his head and began to read, even as the tears rose in his eyes and the page began to blur.

Tuesday, March 24, 1908

Read "Navigating the Air" yesterday and found it intensely interesting. I should like very much to take a trip in a balloon and especially long ones. I did desire that, even when I was a boy (a long time ago) at county fairs or whenever

I saw a balloon ascension. It would be something new, a new experience, and so just suit me. I have enjoyed this confinement for this reason, as it is an entirely new and unusual experience and one that few experience. Then I have a chance to study people under new circumstances. I feel somewhat the same way about death. It will be a condition much different, and I am sure interesting, tho I may not realize that. It will be a change, a development and advance, I hope. Altho I do not want to die, I haven't the fear of it one expects to have.

Charlie shook his head. By this point, Chester would have been on death row for a little over a year. Could that brief amount of time have brought about such a transformation in a young man who had been referred to as immature and self-centered in the past? Hungrily, he read on, even as the date gave him pause. Only four days before the execution.

Thursday, March 26, 1908

"Mac" (MacIlvary) came this morning before I was thru work and I learned that the Governor had decided not to interfere in my case. I was very much surprised, but I hope it was for the best.

Hope it was for the best? That your life would not be spared? That your last hope had just been snuffed out like a candle? Charlie felt like he'd received a blow to the side of his head, the pain piercing through his skull, making him dizzy.

Saturday, March 28, 1908
The "kids" were in this morning early, and so we had a good long visit. Tho it was hard, yet not as hard as I feared, thanks to Paul and the girls. They were all so brave and helpful. I hope I said what would help and encourage them.

There is so much that I want to say, but I can't write it, knowing that others will read it. I have been by myself so much that I find it hard to express my feelings or talk of my deeper thoughts.

What *could* he have said to his brother and sisters? What had Chester withheld even from his own journal, knowing that it would end up in the hands of others? *What about Grace? What am I supposed to tell her? Can you give me nothing, Chester?* Another thought gave him pause…that his ancestor expressed caring about his siblings, the hope that *he* had encouraged them. Not the words of a selfish man. Charlie's hands began to tremble as he looked at the date of the next entry. The last entry. Only hours before Chester's death.

Monday morning, March 30, 1908

Went to bed at 12:30 and was asleep in a few minutes. I slept soundly until called at 3:45. Feel refreshed and calm. I am surprised that I can look at this matter so calmly. Had communion for the first time. I feel that I am fully prepared to go and meet Jesus. I shall watch for the others. Was so glad when Mac told me that Paul had taken a stand for Christ. This makes me happier than anything else could have done. May the rest be comforted as I have been in these last moments. Had a very nice little breakfast and appreciate everyone's kindness. They have all been so kind and courteous. I am very grateful to each one. Good morning All.

P.S. If it isn't any extra expense and too much trouble, please have "Taps" played at the last.

Gone to be with Jesus…

— *Chester*

Charlie's knees gave out and he leaned against the table, Marvin taking the journal so that he could catch himself. His breath came out in a sob, and he clamped down on his lip to contain his emotions. Chester had been so calm, so accepting of his fate. *I will watch for the others.* Did the condemned man mean he would wait for his family? Did they play "Taps"? *Please, God. Let them have played it. Let him be home, with You.* Charlie didn't care what anyone told him. Chester Gillette was no monster. He leaned on the table and covered his eyes with one hand, fighting for composure.

Marvin quietly replaced the journal and closed the lid. He set a hand on Charlie's back and patted him gently. "It's powerful, isn't it? I've read those last entries many times myself. I feel that they are the most telling of all, the words Chester wrote while on the brink of death. Most of us do not have that luxury—to know when our hour is coming, to prepare ourselves to meet our fate. I truly believe that Chester Gillette went to that chair with a clean conscience. I do not know whether he murdered Grace Brown or not, but he atoned for her death in his final days and in his sacrifice. He believed that Jesus was waiting for him, if that gives you any comfort. I'll leave you alone to give you some privacy. The copies are on my desk. You may let yourself out at any time."

Any time? Chester hadn't had that option. The possibility of a reprieve had been dangled before him four days before his death only to be told no. They gave him a nice breakfast, for God's sake. The hypocrisy! Why? To make themselves feel better for what they were about to do? The executioners…they were murderers, too. No one could argue otherwise. They believed Chester's death was justified, but they killed him just the same as his spiritual advisers told the world that there was no wrongdoing in sending the accused on that lonely walk down death row.

Charlie dashed the tears from his face and turned to grab the folder off the librarian's desk. He had to get out of the small, enclosed space, his mind too full of Chester's final moments. He couldn't stop picturing a dingy cell and the terrifying trip to that awful chair. How'd he do it? How was it possible to walk to his death without begging, pleading, and falling to pieces?

Marvin waved a hand from across the library as Charlie headed for the door. He nodded in return but could not manage more. Talk to anyone in that place, and he would break. He rushed out to the car and slid behind the wheel. *I am so done with all of this.*

Finish it. The hair rose up on his back. It was nearly eighty degrees outside, but his car was like an ice chamber. Charlie glanced out of the corner of his eye. Chester was riding shotgun.

I don't want to do it. Go the final mile of Chester's life. To Auburn prison, where his ancestor's feet walked down death row and never walked this earth again.

10

THE DRIVE ONLY TOOK A HALF HOUR. Charlie sat in the parking lot at the Auburn Correctional Facility, staring at the foreboding building under the watchful gaze of Copper John, the Revolutionary soldier statue perched on top. Charlie's collar choked him, and he'd broken out in a cold sweat despite the eighty-degree day. He unbuttoned his top button, then the next, and drew in a deep breath. Nothing helped.

He couldn't erase the image of Old Sparky, the electric chair that used to deliver justice in this facility. The thought of Chester walking his final mile to that dreadful death wrapped itself in a fist around Charlie's heart, squeezing it tightly. This was no longer a research assignment. This was the end of a man's life, a man who had become all too real to him. Leaning his head against the wheel, he heard the words echo in his mind again. *Finish it.*

Finish what, Chester? I can't even find your grave! Charlie fumbled with his phone and punched in Chester's name. The Soule Cemetery was in Auburn, ten minutes away. As had happened so many times, the car found its way; Charlie stepped out, leaning against a gate. He felt unable to go on. The grave site was unmarked. Chester had been abandoned by his family in the end. They hadn't arranged a proper burial.

Charlie staggered to the grass and dropped down on his hands and knees, breathing hard, on the verge of being sick. "I'm sorry, Chester. Your own family turned their backs on you. They could've at least marked your grave site." He swallowed hard and raised his head. In the distance, leaning against a tree, was a dark figure—one he had come to know too well. "I forgive you, Chester. Whatever happened that day, I forgive you."

The ghostly figure turned and looked at him with such sorrow. *Tell Grace.* Charlie understood. It wasn't *his* forgiveness that Chester wanted. The only person who had the power to forgive him was Grace Mae Brown. Charlie stood up and shouted, "How, Chester? How do I find Grace?" The figure vanished.

KATHERINE TAPPED HER FOOT BENEATH THE TABLE, WAITING FOR MIKE. Her black dress was hot, her feet were killing her from heels that were too high, and her forehead hurt because her hair was pulled back too tightly. *Come on! Let's get this over with!* "Can't we just proceed? He doesn't need me to be here to sign his name." Leave it to Michael Graciano to make her wait again. All part of the games he played as a control freak.

Not this time. I'm in the driver's seat! She stood up only to have her lawyer, John Larson, take her hand. "You need to be patient, Katherine. If you don't do this together, with witnesses, you'll have to come back. Might as well get it right the first time." He poured her coffee and patted her back. She wanted to throw her cup against the wall. Instead, she sank back down in her chair, her hands twisting around each other in her lap.

The attorney on the other side of the table, an oily-looking sort, shuffled his papers and stood. "I have more appointments today. My client's a half hour late. I suggest we reschedule."

Katherine jumped to her feet, trembling. "I am *not* rescheduling. This has to happen. *Now.*"

"Chill, Kat. Don't get your panties in a bunch." Mike walked in, looking put together in a dark suit, his blond hair trimmed and slicked back. His eyes were ice cold as he stared at her, his mouth curling in a grin. *Playing cat and mouse with me...yet again.*

"Mr. Graciano, I'll remind you to speak to my client with respect." John was on his feet, his hands planted on the surface of the table. He was just as tall as Mike and could be intimidating.

Mike's attorney whispered something in his ear, to which her soon-to-be ex nodded. His smile grew wider and he cleared his throat. "Absolutely, counselor. My apologies. I want this over as much as you do." Again, he pinned Katherine with his gaze. She resisted the urge to squirm in her chair.

The lawyers got down to business, and the papers made the rounds for signing. Katherine held her breath, expecting the worst at any moment: a mountain of legal documents ripped in half. Furniture tossed against the glass. People thrown this way and that as her worst nightmare clambered over the table to get to her. But nothing happened. Mike signed the last document that was then passed on to Katherine. Damn her hands for shaking. With one palm pressed to her stomach, she managed to sign on the dotted line.

Mike stood up and shook hands with her attorney, then his own. "Thank you, gentlemen. High time *that* was over. Come on, Anthony. I know a good bar where I can buy you a drink to celebrate my freedom." He slung an arm around his lawyer's shoulders, and they headed out the door. At the last moment, he glanced over his shoulder and caught Katherine's eye. *It's not over,* he mouthed silently.

Yes, it most definitely is. You are yesterday's news. Katherine didn't give him the satisfaction of a response. She gathered her copies of her papers, thanked her lawyer, and went out to her car. As soon as she was in the driver's seat, she locked the door and kicked off her shoes. Massaging her aching feet, she stared up at the ceiling. It was finally, truly done.

Katherine sagged against the steering wheel and let out the breath she'd been holding all morning. No more Mike. No more looking over her shoulder. Maybe the dreams and strange visions would subside now. After all, stress did do terrible things to the mind and body. *There's one more thing you have to do.* She sat up and punched in an address on her phone, letting the GPS lead the way.

SOUTH OTSELIC WAS A QUIET TOWN ABOUT AN HOUR OUTSIDE OF SYRACUSE. It was Grace Mae Brown's hometown. Katherine welcomed the distance between the courthouse and the Valley View Cemetery. It helped her unwind. She took the time to pick up flowers in a convenience store along the way and a bracelet with *Billy* engraved on it. Grace had loved Billy the Kid and had signed many of her letters as "Kid."

The directions made it easy to find Grace's family plot and a small, unassuming stone that was surrounded by her relatives, including her mother and father. Grace had been the first member of the family to go. Katherine walked through the grass in her stocking feet; otherwise, she was sure she'd twist an ankle walking through the aisles of stones. She knelt by Grace's stone and skimmed her fingers over the granite. Nothing happened. No chills. No images. No voices. Relieved, she paid her respects, laying the flowers on the grass and draping the bracelet over them. "Rest in peace, Grace. It's over. Let him go."

She sat there at least a half hour, listening to the wind in the trees, letting it kiss her skin. Katherine felt peaceful for the first time in a long time. Perhaps Grace's soul would finally be at ease, too. She stood up and blew a kiss, turning back to make her way to her car. No one walked with her. No woman in white wandered between the markers, yet she felt like a hand pressed gently on the middle of her back. *Go home.* Katherine wiped her face and nodded as she turned on the ignition. Right now, Ward's Pond was the closest thing to home that she had.

CHARLIE PULLED INTO THE PARKING AREA AT THE BED AND BREAKFAST. For a few minutes, he didn't move, his eyes closed. He didn't want to see Chester—or anyone else at that moment. All he wanted to do was go to bed, sleep, and forget the whole thing. *That's not happening, and you know it.*

He stepped out of the car, his sleeves rolled up to his elbow, his jacket and pack slung over his shoulder. After a few steps toward the porch, he saw Katherine sitting by the pond, as was her habit. A glance beyond revealed the ghostly image of a boat carrying a man and woman dressed in the clothing of a bygone era. The night was warm, but he shivered. The date stood out in his mind: July 9th. Two days to the anniversary of Grace Brown's death, the day that would set the ball rolling and lead to an execution…

Charlie kept his head down and turned away from the pond, intent on reaching his room, maybe drinking himself to oblivion. He would not look out on that water. No matter what he had discovered in all his searching and digging for the truth, the end was always the same and irrevocable. Grace, dead, in the water over 110 years ago—or just the other day if you counted the vision he and Katherine shared. His feet moved faster, picking up the pace, when someone stepped in front of him, blocking his path.

"Charlie, look at me." Katherine made him jerk to a halt, but still, he wouldn't look, fearful of what he'd see.

She put her hand under his jaw and forced his eyes to meet hers. They glittered in the moonlight. "You all right?"

His jaw went tight, his hands balling into fists. *Grace. Tell Grace.* Chester's voice echoed in his mind. If he looked at the pond, he'd be forced to watch all over again, and the undercurrent of dread that had been with him for days threatened to smother him. "I'm fine. Just tired. It's been a long day. For you as well, I'm sure. Why don't we talk in the morning, Katherine? I just want to go lie down for a while."

Her hands moved to his cheeks. They were warm and soft. Here. Now. "You know what we both need? We need to put the past behind us and embrace the future...a future I see with you in it." Katherine stepped in closer and placed her lips on his. His hands trailed up her waist, the fine lines of her ribs, then to her head, cupping it and threading his fingers into her hair. Pushing aside all other thoughts and ghostly encounters, Charlie simply couldn't get enough of her.

It was like *he* was drowning in that pond and *she* was his lifeline, the very air that he breathed. Charlie rested his head on hers, both panting, hearts hammering against one another. "I see that too, Katherine. I want to move forward, too. God, you don't know how much I want that. I just can't seem to get past this story."

"We can...together. That's where Chester and Grace went wrong." Hand in hand, they walked to the house. Charlie didn't look back...and Chester no longer walked with him. Perhaps today, his work was done.

Eva greeted them at the door. "Charlie, you have a visitor. She said she was interested in your work."

They stepped into the parlor to find an elderly woman sitting on the couch. She was dressed in black and bore severe features, her steel-gray hair twisted into a tight bun. She stared intently at Charlie with eyes like slate through wire-framed glasses perched on the end of her nose. As he approached, she drew herself to her feet. She was diminutive but still had a powerful presence about her. "Charlie Baxter?" she inquired.

Katherine stood back by Eva to give them privacy, allowing Charlie to greet his guest, his hand extended. "May I help you?"

She stepped closer, fire flashing in her eyes. "I'm Ida Mae Brown, Grace Brown's great-grandniece." Her hand drew back, and she slapped him in the face, hard enough to make tears spring to his eyes. Taken by surprise, Charlie stepped back, but she pushed on, wagging a finger too close for comfort and jabbing it in the center of his chest.

"I read about your upcoming book in the *New York Times*, Mr. Baxter, your quest for the *truth*. Haven't you Gillettes done enough?" She bit off every word, spitting them out. "Yes, I know who you are. I can see Chester in you, in your hair, the tilt of your head, the way you carry yourself. He was cocky, too, so puffed up and sure of himself. Look where that got *him!* You need to let Grace be, God rest her soul. Gillette was a murderer. Nothing you do or say is going to wipe that stain from your blood."

"I think you've said enough." Katherine stepped forward and took Charlie's hand.

Charlie couldn't stop shaking. How could he have been so naïve? There was no escaping his past.

Eva joined them, her shoulders set, chin raised. "I'd like you to leave, Ms. Brown. *Now*, please. I'll not have you harassing my guest. You are *not* welcome here." The small gypsy of a hostess escorted Ms. Brown to the door and locked it, pressing her back up against it to catch her breath.

Charlie collapsed into a chair, Katherine massaging his neck, his shoulders, and his back as his head dropped in his hands. Eva hugged him on her way to the kitchen. "Sorry, Charlie. I'd no idea." She bustled off, returning with a towel and ice for his cheek.

Katherine held it for him. "She left the mark of her hand in flaming red, she slapped you so hard. That must really sting."

"Not as much as her words." His breath came out in one long sigh. "I thought after today I'd have closure, going to see Chester's journal, the prison, his cemetery. It's like I opened Pandora's box when I started digging into the past. What have I unleashed? I don't know if I can ever get away from this case, Katherine."

She sat down beside him and rested her hand on the nape of his neck. "I felt that way, too. When I went to sign those papers today, Mike didn't show up until a half hour after our appointed time. His lawyer almost left. I know he did it on purpose, but it doesn't matter. It *is* over and done with, Charlie. I'm officially not married."

Charlie sat up and took her hand, setting aside his troubles. "I'm glad to hear that, Katherine. Are you happy?"

She laughed softly. "So happy, I celebrated by bringing flowers to Grace. It seemed like the right thing to do." She leaned forward to move the ice aside. "That's much better. Let me see what else I can do." With that, Katherine skimmed her lips over his cheek. Her phone rang, making them both jump.

"Sorry." She glanced down at the number. "It's my mother." Katherine stood and walked to the windows. "Mom, what's going on?" Something made Charlie follow her. Standing next to her, his arm wrapped around her, he could hear the speaker on the other end. A man. An angry man whose controlled, level tone made it all the more frightening.

"You think today means it's over? That's just a piece of paper, Katherine, and I know where you are." There was a woman's shriek as the phone crashed on the floor, the slamming of a door, and the revving of a car engine, followed by the sound of squealing tires.

There was a fumbling with the phone and then a tearful voice. "Oh, Katherine, I'm so sorry, honey. He came in here and knocked me down, said it would be worse for you if I didn't tell him. He's on his way there now, baby. So run! Run while you can!"

Katherine hit the *End call* button and whipped around. Charlie could see the terror in her eyes, and in that moment, everything made sense. That day at the Violet Festival. Her bruised wrist. The miscarriage.

Charlie's stomach gave a lurch. "Katherine...did Mike...did he make you lose your baby?"

She ducked her head, her hair becoming a curtain. Her voice was low, so soft he could hardly hear her. "He came home drunk. It was only when Mike was drunk that he became nasty. I found that out the hard way. He pushed me. I fell down the stairs and I lost her. Lost Daisy. That's why I had to end it between us. It was bad enough that he hurt me...but our baby?" Her voice broke on the last.

Charlie pushed her hair aside and pressed his palm to her cheek. "I'm so sorry, Katherine, so sorry that someone hurt you like this." *What if Chester actually did the same to Grace?* The thought made him sick to his stomach.

Katherine pulled away and moved toward the stairs. "I have to leave before he gets here. I guess I was wrong, Charlie. My past isn't ready to let go, either."

He sprinted in front of her to block her path. "No, we'll face him. Together. Like you said. You can't run forever, Katherine. You need to deal with him—now—and I'll help you."

Charlie locked the doors first, front and back, hurrying off to warn Eva that they might have another unwelcome visitor. They checked all the windows on every floor, making sure they were latched, and the blinds were down, or the curtains closed. Finally, Katherine sat in the parlor in a chair tucked in the corner, someplace where Mike wouldn't see her right away, practically hidden. Charlie waited with her.

Sometime after midnight, headlights appeared in the driveway as tires rolled over the gravel, making it crunch. The hum of the motor died, and a car door slammed. Heavy footsteps approached. Through the parking lot. Down the path. Up the steps. To the door. A loud pounding began, followed by shouting. "Katherine! I'm here to take what's mine, and that's you. In the eyes of the church, you are bound to me. Forever. Open up, Kat! Don't make me hurt you!"

Eva poked her head out of her quarters while Charlie stood with his back pressed to the door, waiting for the battering ram. "Eva, lock yourself in your apartment and call nine-one-one. Do it. *Now.*"

The shouting and the pounding grew louder, followed by heavy footsteps across the porch and then the shattering of glass in the parlor. Charlie ran in to see a mountain of a man climbing through the opening, heedless of the cuts on his arms and face. Katherine had said he was an ex-marine, and it showed. Her ex-husband was solid. Mean. Terrifying. Especially to a little thing like Katherine. Mike spotted her and lunged for her chair. Charlie threw himself at him like a linebacker, taking him down to the floor.

Mike was up in an instant and the fight began, with both men swinging at each other, grunting and crying out. Charlie was on the losing end of the deal when it came to size, but he made up for it in determination, running at his opponent, wrapping his arms around him, and plowing him down. They continued to throw punches at each other, neither getting anywhere except bloodied and bruised, when someone burst through the door.

"Police! That's enough! Both of you, on your feet. Hands in the air. Don't make another move or I'll charge you with resisting an arrest." The officer moved forward, cuffs in hand, another officer flanking him.

Katherine fled from her corner toward one of the officers. "The blond one is the problem, officers. We had divorce proceedings today. He wasn't happy." Both officers turned their attention to Mike while she took Charlie's arm and led him to the couch.

The blood was dripping from his nose, a cut on his mouth, and his cheek. Charlie winked at her, something that wasn't hard to do with his swollen eye. "Do I look pretty?" She burst into tears.

11

"*I DON'T THINK THIS PLACE HAS EVER SEEN THIS MUCH EXCITEMENT.*" Eva dabbed at Charlie's cuts and handed him an ice pack for the second time in one night. Katherine couldn't stop crying. The caring hostess set a hand on her shoulder. "It's over, sweetie. You've given your statement and pressed charges. From what you said he did to you, plus violating his restraint order, he's going away."

Katherine nodded but felt like she was beginning to unravel. She swiped at her face with her sleeve and glanced around the room. "I'm sorry about your window. I can pay for it. If you'll show me where your broom and dustpan is, I'll clean up…"

Eva gave her a hug. "Honey, homeowner's insurance will cover the window, and I'll take care of the glass. Why don't you take care of Charlie?" She jutted her chin his way. His eye was nearly swollen shut, his lip puffy, and he'd started to sway. It *was* two in the morning by then.

Katherine went to his chair and took his hand. "Come on, Charlie. It's past your bedtime." He gave her a crooked grin and stood up, wavering on his feet. She ducked under his shoulder and brought him up to his room, helping him to stretch out on his bed. "How do you feel?"

"My ribs hurt, and my back, and my shoulder. I don't even want to talk about my face. I guess I'll never be a prizefighter." He reached up to stroke her cheek as she sat by him on the edge of the bed. "The more important question is, how are you?"

The tears sprang up once more. "Still a little shaky, but it's finally over. Because of you." She bent forward and kissed him gently, avoiding his poor swollen lip. "Sweet dreams."

He reached for her and held her hand. "Stay. With me. I don't want you to be alone. I promise I won't do anything. I don't even think I could if I tried. I don't want to be alone, either." Slowly, Charlie rolled onto his side and gently stroked her hair. "I know you're scared, but you don't ever have to be afraid of me. Everything is going to be all right."

Wordlessly, she stretched out beside him as the moonlight streaked through the window. Her eyes drooped shut. She was so tired, but Charlie made her feel safe. Katherine lay very still, waiting for her heart to slow down, listening to the breathing of the man beside her until it finally fell into an easy rhythm. Only then did sleep come for her.

HE WAS BURNING UP FROM THE INSIDE OUT, everything sizzling. Popping. Hissing. Fire was running through his veins, the smell of smoke making him choke; he started to jerk uncontrollably, his teeth clacking together. His nerves and muscles were screaming with a pain like nothing else he'd experienced in his life. A sound like an animal in agony rose up from his gut, up and up, clawing its way out of his mouth...and his heart exploded like a stake ran him through.

"Charlie! Oh God, Charlie, please wake up! You made the most horrible sound. Charlie, please!"

Someone was shaking him, tears falling on his face and forcing him back up to the surface, rescuing him from the depths of his nightmare.

He opened his eyes, and relief washed over him. For one awful moment, he thought a blindfold was covering the top half of his face like in the dream. It was just the cloak of darkness in the middle of the night. In his familiar room at Ward's Pond. Far removed from the Auburn Correctional Facility and an appointment with death. Charlie gulped a great gasp of air and started to cough.

Someone stood by his bed. He looked up and thought he saw the slight figure of Grace Brown until Katherine touched him. A lighthouse in the tempest. She was trembling and pale in the moonlight, wearing a white nightgown with her hair pulled away from her face. Her eyes were wide with fright, but her hand grabbed hold of his with a tenacious grip. Charlie had absolute faith. She would not let go.

His heart continued to hammer in his chest, so hard it hurt. He dragged in one deep breath, and then another. "We've got to stop meeting this way," Charlie whispered faintly.

Katherine pulled her hand back as if it had been bitten. "You're freezing! Your hands are like ice!" She reached for the glass of water by the bed with trembling fingers and set it in his, only to hold on when it started to slosh over the side. He was none too steady himself.

Finally, he drank some down and whispered hoarsely, "Thank you."

"What was it, Charlie? What did you dream?" She sank onto the mattress and rested her palm on his cheek, offering comfort and strength.

He shook his head and leaned back, covering his eyes with his arm. "It was a nightmare, a wretched nightmare. I was on fire...from the inside out."

"Like Chester," she whispered, the horror he felt echoing in her words.

He shuddered at the thought. If that was actually what his ancestor felt, God help the man. Death by electrocution was barbaric, and Charlie would be sure to protest anywhere in the land once his mission was accomplished. If he survived it.

"He's...always with me. *All the time*. I can put him in the back of my mind, but he's still there. Like a nagging toothache that won't ever go away. You know how you told me to walk in his shoes? I never expected to walk death row with him." Charlie cut himself off, holding on tightly to Katherine's hand as a dreadful thought popped unbidden into his mind. "Is it like that for you with Grace?"

"No. I've only seen her a few times...and then she's gone. The pond and the first dream—that night I arrived here—those were the only times that I felt like I *was* Grace. Chester is with you *all* the time?"

"God help me, yes. Ever since I started researching the Gillette-Brown murder." The entire bed was shaking. He couldn't stop. Why? Why did his mother have to lead him down this path? *Why did Chester Gillette have to be my ancestor?*

Katherine slipped under the covers and pressed up against him. "You're all right. You're going to be all right." She reached up and stroked hair from his face before resting her palm on his chest. "Your heart is racing."

Charlie set his trembling hand on hers and let out a breath he didn't know had been trapped inside of him. "Just hold me. Make me forget." She laid her head on his shoulder.

"Promise you won't go," he whispered raggedly.

"I'm not going anywhere. I promise." Katherine snuggled in closer, making herself a second skin or a bandage to hold back the inevitable. If she wasn't there, he'd bleed out.

Hours later, after staring up at the ceiling for a long time, reliving a dream he'd much rather forget in detail so vivid it felt undeniably real, Charlie's body finally surrendered to sleep. And Katherine was still there come morning.

SHE FOUND HIM BY THE POND. After a night like he had, Katherine feared he'd jump in with a heavy weight chained to his ankles. That gruesome image sent a shudder right through her, and she rushed to his bench. When she couldn't find him inside after her shower, she searched the house high and low. Ward's Pond should have been the first place she looked.

Taking a deep breath, she steeled herself and walked out to join him. Ever since her night of sleepwalking, it had stopped being one of her favorite spots at the bed and breakfast, but she could not leave him alone with his thoughts. It was a much too dangerous place to be, where he could be shipwrecked, dashed amongst the jagged rocks of guilt and self-doubt. If Charlie sank into depression, Katherine wasn't sure she could pull him out.

He sat with his elbows on his knees, his head in his hands. He glanced up when she sank down beside him only to look away, but not before revealing the face of a tortured soul. "I've been thinking about what you said one day, that some bones have to stay buried. This one won't stay buried. It just keeps getting unearthed, coming for me. I'm afraid it will take me down with it."

Katherine rested her hand on his shoulder, a solid presence when everything else seemed to be spiraling out of control. "I think you're meant to finally put Chester and Grace to rest, to give them peace. Don't they deserve it after all these years? You can't quit now. Stop doing it for yourself or your family. Do it for them, Charlie."

He stood up fast and gazed out over the water, the heat rising in his face, his voice starting to shake. "None of it has done any good on this wild goose chase! Coming here, to Judge Ward's house, going to all the places they stayed—from Cortland to Old Forge, to the Auburn Correctional Facility where he died...and...Chester's journal? That...*that was torture. Like being skinned alive.*"

He couldn't go on. Katherine stood up from the bench and went to him, wrapping her arms around his waist. "What about the journal?"

"I felt like I was in his head with every page I read, sucked in deeper with each entry, and I still didn't get any answers. I started thinking about Chester. He was only twenty-three when he landed in a mess of trouble, Katherine! *Twenty-three!* Nearly ten years younger than I am. Grace was twenty. They were practically kids, so confused about everything. My ancestor had a screwed-up life. Going from a life of privilege to the exact opposite when his parents went full-swing religious, they gave up everything. When he went to the skirt factory with his uncle, Chester started mingling with upper-crust members of society in the evening and on weekends, but he stood side by side with poor workers every day. He was caught in a tug-of-war. He must have been so torn, but I don't believe Chester killed her."

"Maybe he didn't. Tell me what you've learned." Katherine took his hand and led him back to sit down by the pond.

Charlie shook his head. "Nothing definitive. Just a feeling, deep down in my gut, you know? Killing Grace doesn't make sense! She had a suitcase filled with enough stuff to go to a home for unwed mothers, maybe up in Saranac Lake. It's true that Chester used a fake name as they went on their journey, but he used his own name in Inlet where he was waiting for his mail. Why would he do that if he was planning on getting rid of her? Maybe he only used fake names when they were together, to keep both of them out of trouble."

Katherine nodded. "Maybe it wasn't premeditation. Chester could have been covering their tracks to protect both of them. No one needed to know about the trouble Grace was in. People's views were a lot less understanding about pregnancy out of wedlock back then, not to mention a factory worker getting involved with the boss's nephew. Once Chester got her to the home for unwed mothers, he'd need to go back to his normal life."

Charlie grabbed her hand, animated for the first time since the dream. "Was it right that he wouldn't stand by her with the baby and marry her? No, but what kind of life would they have had back then?

He would have lost his job and been brought down to nothing all over again. That happened to Chester too many times. He wouldn't have wanted to go down that road again."

All the more reason to kill her, the insidious voice inside his head hissed, and Charlie felt singed by the fire in his veins once again. He caught his breath and argued back in a mental battle of the wills. *Well, he paid for it, didn't he? Intentional or no, Chester burned.* He squeezed his eyes shut and swallowed hard. His dream only gave an inkling of what his ancestor felt the day he surrendered his life. He'd done more than burn. He'd been torched from the inside out.

Katherine pressed his hand. "Charlie, are you all right? You've gone awfully pale."

He remained silent. In his mind's eye, Charlie could see the neat script of Chester's journal. He met Katherine's troubled gaze, desperate to make her understand. "Read his journal and you'll see that it's the words of someone much older than his twenty-four years, I'll tell you that. Chester aged a lifetime while he waited for a little over a year in that cell to die. He never publicly admitted guilt, not in his final statement or letters, not even in the privacy of his own journal. He came to terms with what he had done to his family, if anything…and that dream…" Charlie pressed his hands to his head. "God, that dream…I can't get it out of my head!"

Katherine leaned against him, her cheek pressed to his shoulder, arms around him, holding on. "I really don't know, Charlie. You have to accept that you may never have the answers you seek."

He rested his head on hers and let out a ragged sigh. "I'm sorry. I'm just so damned tired and spread too thin. I know my problems aren't real, not like yours. Hell, this case happened over a hundred years ago, but it's eating me up inside. I wish my mother had never told me about it."

Katherine met his gaze even though it hurt to look at the pain rising in his eyes. "You're trying to find the truth—whatever that may be—for someone who *is* a part of your family, like it or not. It's brave of you to stand up against the established beliefs and risk finding out something you'd rather not know. I know you're tired, but it'll be worth it in the end…and I'll help you finish it. My marriage is officially over; I have no strings attached and no place to go. My calendar is wide open."

Charlie's head tilted down, and his lips skimmed her hair. "I just want this story to let me go." He started to sway and pressed a hand to his temple. "Whoa. I've got to go lie down before I fall down."

Katherine made sure he made it to his bed. She drew the blinds, pulled up the covers, and kissed him gently. "Get some sleep, Charlie. That could be exactly what you need."

SLEEP. WHAT WAS THAT? At two in the morning, he sat up quickly, pulled out of a nightmare. The smell of smoke still surrounded him, and a splitting headache drove him in search of aspirin. Charlie picked up the journal and started reading it again from the beginning, in depth. He took notes, hoping to find something that he had overlooked. Some hidden meaning in his ancestor's words. Something to give his mother solace. To give Grace justice. To give Charlie peace. The hands on the clock ticked by, daylight bled into the room, and still— he was getting…nowhere.

He smacked his hand on the table when someone knocked softly at the door. "Room service."

"Come in," he called out, attempting to create some semblance of order on his desk. Katherine walked in with coffee and a plate heaped with food. "I figured this was what you were doing when I didn't see your face this morning. You should have been a detective. Do you know it's almost noon?"

"No, I had no idea. Thanks for reinforcements." He dragged his hands over his face, the stubble of his beard scraping against his skin as rough as sandpaper. Charlie grabbed hold of the unraveling bits of his soul and raised his cup to her as if in a toast. He took a swallow, eating distractedly with a pen behind his ear. All the while, his mind kept running itself ragged, but he dared not stop. He dared not sleep, or the chair might take him again. He feared another trip down death row, real or no, would be the end of him. The dark turn of his thoughts sent a shudder racing through him. Charlie closed his eyes and gripped the edge of the desk until his knuckles bulged. A hand rested on his neck. Fearing it might be Chester or Grace, he slowly peeked out from the slit of one eyelid.

Katherine glanced over his shoulder, making him sag forward in relief. She read Chester's final entries surrounded by hastily scrawled notes. Her eyes started to tear up as her hand went to her mouth. "Oh, Charlie! How terrible."

He felt as if the color was draining from his face, a chill washing over him. "That last one? Those are his final words." He closed the laptop with hands that trembled. "I think that triggered the nightmare. It really shook me up."

Katherine took the cup and plate away, sitting down in his lap. She didn't talk, simply let him have his purge of sorts.

"When I first came here…I saw Chester from time to time. Sometimes, I thought I heard him…but *now*? I feel like he's inside of me, and it's terrifying…because he really is." Charlie bit off a curse and ran a hand through his hair. "I grew up hearing this story in hushed tones, how my family was disgraced by it, even though so many years had passed. I even avoided getting involved with anyone because I thought…I thought I might be tainted in some way by sharing his family's blood, that I might hurt someone…" His throat closed and he choked up at the thought.

Katherine placed her hands on his face and gave him a little shake. "Charlie, look at me! *Look at me*! *You* could not hurt anyone. It's like you told me. *You* are not, Chester. He has just chosen you to tell his side of the story."

He ran his hands through his hair. "I don't think so! I think he wants me to apologize to Grace, ask for forgiveness. How can I possibly do that? He can't bring her back, can't make up for a life cut short."

Katherine set her hand under his chin and pressed until he met her steady gaze. He could see a miniature reflection of himself in her eyes. Pale. Drawn from a restless night, with dark smudges under his eyes. Charlie refused to look up to the spot on the wall where the judgmental eyes of George Ward surveyed everything in his surroundings in a smaller version of the downstairs portrait. He closed his eyes until Katherine moved in, and her mouth met his. "I think you have to finish it, Charlie. You need to go the distance, all the way to Inlet...and Big Moose Lake."

12

THE HEADACHE BLOOMED AT THE BASE of his skull, pounding the moment he opened his eyes, picking up in intensity until it hammered the walls of his brain. Charlie closed his eyes, breathed in deeply, and let it out. He reached back to massage his neck when he heard the screen door creak open, then swing shut. The scent of something floral—heavenly, really—made him dizzy. That was nothing compared to Katherine's touch.

Her skin was cool and soothing, gently taking over a badly needed massage as her hands drove into muscles gone tight, eventually making them go loose. It felt like a current of electricity was sizzling through his veins every time her touch connected with his. *Like Chester and Grace.* If it was anything like Charlie felt in Katherine's hands, there'd have been no contest. They would have had to give in to each other, class barriers be damned.

Resisting the urge to pull her into his arms and ravish Katherine on the spot, Charlie caught his breath, took a sip of his coffee, and reached back to lay his hand on hers. She was the picture of calm. Normal. What Charlie so badly wanted to be. What he'd never been and he suspected he never would be.

"Good morning." Something prompted him to act like gentlemen in days of old. He grazed his lips over her fingers.

Katherine walked in front of him, pressed her palm beneath his chin, and forced him to look at her. She winced. "Still a rough night? Why don't you go back to bed for a while?"

He couldn't tell her that the thought of going to sleep was terrifying. All he had to do was close his eyes and Charlie was sitting in that chair, high voltage coursing through him, making all the hair on his body start to smoke. The scent burned in his nostrils and nearly made him sick to his stomach.

He shook his head to clear it of that horrifying image, laughing half-heartedly. "No. I can't face whatever kind of crazy my dream world wants to throw at me right now. I just have to get out of here for a bit, okay? Want to come?"

"Where are we going?"

"Inlet. It's the last place Chester went on that tragic journey until he was sent to prison. Maybe that town can tell us something that no place else could." Charlie shied away from the place where two lives were cut short, where Grace Mae Brown lost her life—Big Moose Lake.

KATHERINE DIDN'T QUESTION HIM, JUST PACKED AN OVERNIGHT BAG—just in case—and sat down in the passenger seat of the car. She put her complete faith and trust in him.

Standing on the porch at Ward's Pond, staring at her sweet face, Charlie found himself suddenly overcome with dizziness, exhaustion catching up with him. The crash could not be far off in the future. *Just hang on a little bit longer. You're almost there and then you can rest. Forever?*

They hit the road. Charlie turned on the radio, cranking up the oldies—anything for a distraction. He planned on procrastinating, taking his time as they ventured through the Adirondacks. If they went deep enough into its heart, they wouldn't ever have to come back. The car had other plans. It pulled him toward their destination.

Grace. Charlie's grip tightened on the wheel. *I know, Chester! Will you just be quiet before you drive me completely out of my mind?* The signs began to appear for Inlet: 40 miles…30 miles…20 miles…10. The closer they came to their destination, the more Charlie wanted to turn the car around and go anywhere but here.

Katherine was animated, bubbling over with enthusiasm as they pulled into the quaint little town, which was bustling with activity. It threw him off, making the questions start to circle in his mind again. If Katherine was connected to Grace in some way, it seemed highly unlikely that she'd find any joy in this place. Sighing deeply, Charlie took her hand as they left the car behind. It might be paranoia, but he was afraid to let go of her.

They walked down the short strip on the main drag that included a clump of shops, poking their heads in sporadically, stopping to window-shop at others, gazing at the wares that were on display. Every time they saw their reflection, Charlie was terrified that he'd see Chester again, but his ancestor made no appearance. Not yet.

Making a desperate effort at normal, Charlie gestured to a tiny bakery tucked beneath a gift shop. "You hungry?"

Katherine clapped her hands together, her smile wide and irresistible. "I thought you would never ask. I am starving, and those humongous cupcakes have my name on them. The one with peanut butter frosting, please."

Charlie laughed and nodded to the owner. "I'll take two of the sinful cupcakes with peanut butter frosting and a couple bottles of old-fashioned soda."

With the baked goods in hand, they headed back to the sidewalk, enjoying every morsel of gooey goodness. Katherine tipped her head back in the sunshine to take a swallow of black cherry soda and took Charlie's breath away. His hand came up to push a strand of her hair behind her ear as they passed through the entrance of Arrowhead Park, where two stone light towers stood guard, and they headed toward the water. In his mind, he pictured old photos of the Arrowhead Hotel standing over the lake, the hotel where Chester fled after Grace went into Big Moose Lake—whether accidentally or maliciously.

Charlie touched one of the stone columns and felt like he was being caught in high tide, sweeping him away, carrying him back. The scene shifted. It wasn't a park anymore. He was rocking in a boat and Grace stood in the bow, agitated, wringing her hands. "What about the baby, Chester? Our baby? I can't give it up! I can't live without you! What do I do?"

The boat started to pitch, like Charlie had dreamed before. He stood up, but it only made things worse. She fell, her head making a sickening thud against the side before she went under. "Gracie!"

He called out in a voice that wasn't his own; it was Chester's, the voice that had been his companion since he set foot in the bed and breakfast on Ward's Pond. Fear and desperation coursed through him. His heart was pounding, a cold sweat drenching him. He lunged forward and tried to catch Grace even as a ghostly hand rose from the dark waters only to sink down, out of sight.

The boat rocked violently, tipping him overboard. Everything went with him. His hat, his suitcase, the tennis racket. He started fighting for his own life, going under, sobbing and struggling to make his way back up to the surface again. A cloud of dread wrapped itself around him. *What have I done? What do I do now?*

Panicked, he made his way to shore and pulled himself out of the water. Stumbling, his feet carried him through the woods, branches slapping at his face and snagging his clothes. *Gracie is dead and you couldn't save her! You useless coward!* The words kept beating against his skull.

Eventually, he found his way out, playing the biggest acting role of his life when he pretended that absolutely nothing was wrong. It was clumsy, really, to fall in the lake that way. All the while, his mind spun. *You called yourself Carl Grahm of Albany at the Glenmore Hotel. No one knows you're Chester Gillette.*

In that instant, the pain doubled him over. He thought about Grace as he sat in his room in the Arrowhead Hotel, his head in his hands, picturing her lost in the cold, lonely depths of the lake. A sorrow and despair so deep swallowed him in a gaping pit with no way out. He grieved. For the destruction of Grace's life...and his own. For the hard-won knowledge that he loved her—a secret he would keep all the way to the grave. There was a loud pounding on his door, and the police burst in. It was over.

Charlie came back to himself, one hand pressed to a stone column at Arrowhead Park. Katherine ducked under his arm, shaking him. "Charlie?! Charlie, you're scaring me. Are you having a heart attack? I don't know CPR and cell service is patchy here. I'll have to run for help, but I don't want to leave you. Charlie...*stop scaring me*!" Her voice was rising in pitch, headed for hysteria.

As if in a fog, he thought vaguely that she sounded like Chester. His hand gripped the chilled, rough surface of the light tower beneath his palm. He drew a deep breath and swiped his arm across his forehead, wiping away a cold sweat. He was drenched and began to shiver, even though a hot sun hovered above them.

Charlie sagged against the post for a moment and buried his face in her curls. "Just hold on to me a minute, okay?" His heart hammered against her chest, fit to explode. If it didn't slow down soon, he *would* have a heart attack. Catching a glimpse of Katherine's pulse fluttering madly in her neck, he clamped down on the anxiety crawling inside of him to pull it together. A few deep breaths were enough to steady himself. "I'm all right."

Her face twisted as she snapped, "Really? I don't think so. What happened to you? It's like you were gone. Your body was here, but your mind? No one was home."

Skirting the question for as long as he could, Charlie stammered, "Do you feel anything here?" She stared at him, echoing what he already knew to be true. *You are going completely out of your mind.* Wary, Katherine set her shoulders, her mouth forming a grim line. She closed her eyes and became very still. After a passage of two minutes, Katherine shook her head.

Of course not, Charlie thought to himself. This would not have been Grace's place. She was already dead when Chester fled to Inlet seeking sanctuary...because he killed her or panicked when he failed to save her. Either way, he came alone. Katherine wouldn't have any of Grace's memories to share.

Shakily, he turned, taking a step back toward town. "Let's go, Katherine. There's nothing here. It's just hopeless, all of it." Charlie was an empty husk, as if all his fighting spirit had slipped away. Katherine took his hand, and they walked only a few steps before it felt as if someone grabbed his shoulder. With a force that was almost physical, it whipped him around to see Chester standing by the shore, his eyes mournful. *The truth will set you free...and me, too. Find it, Charlie. You're the only one who can.*

"Find *what*, Chester? *There's nothing here!*" He staggered and nearly fell.

Katherine ducked under his arm, concern making her forehead crinkle. "Charlie, you're scaring me. Let's go get some real food in you; you haven't had anything all day. Then, we are going to find a hotel and you're going to rest. You're running on empty and it's playing tricks on your mind. I'm telling you right now, Chester Gillette is not here."

He didn't argue with her, allowing the woman beside him to take the lead. All the while *Grace* echoed in his head; her name laced with such sorrow it nearly drove him out of his mind. Chester's urgency was growing, and it was going to push Charlie over the brink.

They sat down in a café and placed their order. Something simple. Soup and sandwiches. The words on the menu blurred and Charlie leaned forward, digging his palms into his eyes. Katherine rested her hand on his. "I wish I could help you more with this case, Charlie. Chester Gillette is tearing you apart."

Their waitress, setting their steaming bowls of soup before them, took pause, her eyes lighting up. "Did you just mention the Gillette-Brown murder?" At Katherine's reluctant nod, the woman began to chatter. "I have always been fascinated by that story. Blame it on Old Red. Red Foster is our resident expert on the case. He lives and breathes this story. Any scrap he can find, any rock he can turn over, you can trust that man to pick up on it. He's like a bloodhound."

Charlie set down his spoon at that, straightening up at the prospect of a lead—any lead—looking for Chester's proverbial needle in a haystack. "Does he live nearby?"

The waitress nodded and smiled. "Just over in Raquette Lake. If there's anything to be known about that murder case, Old Red will know it. Just tell him Vera sent you over." Her smile faded as she truly looked at Charlie, and her eyes became dark and troubled. "You eat up, hon. You don't look good." With that, she walked away.

Katherine cleared her throat as Charlie stared off into nothing, his thoughts turned inward. She placed the spoon in his hand and stared at him pointedly. "You heard the woman. Eat before I feed you like a baby. I have a feeling you might need as much fortification as possible before you go see Old Red." She took a few bites of her own soup only to have her mouth quirk up at the corner. "Isn't that the name of a dog in a country song?"

Charlie sputtered at that one, laughing for the first time in days. "Only you would think of such a thing!" Basking in the warmth of her sunny personality, the knot in his gut eased up enough to let him eat. As soon as they were done, he laid the bills out on the table and took Katherine's hand, drawing her with him back to the car. "Okay. Here goes nothing."

She leaned over and kissed his cheek. "It's always something. Especially with you. Every bit of progress you make counts."

13

FORTY MINUTES. FORTY MINUTES TO PREPARE for what might be the end of this road—good or bad. Charlie eyed the sky. It was clear as could be, even as the light began to fade. He almost wished for a horrendous storm, something that would make them turn back, that would wipe away all his memories about this case. Something that would allow him to have a clean slate with the incredible woman in the seat beside him. Ever since the night he crossed the hall when Katherine's nightmare ripped them both from sleep, this dark cloud had hovered over them. Charlie just wanted to banish it for good.

The sign for Raquette Lake told them to turn one mile ahead. At the intersection, the car coasted to a stop. Charlie hit the directional…and didn't move. Katherine touched his arm. He turned and met her encouraging smile. "Go on. You can do this, Charlie, and I'm right here with you."

With a nod, he turned the wheel. The road was winding, wrapping around a small lake with a tiny community situated around its shores. There were hardly any homes or businesses. Just a small pocket of civilization, carving out a niche in the middle of the wilderness. Charlie followed the waitress's directions and pulled up to a house with *Foster* on the mailbox.

It was a shoebox of a house, really, just a tiny cabin with wood siding and cedar shakes for the roof. Nestled against a stand of pines, it was almost as if the place was about to merge with the forest and become one. Let the trees grow a bit taller, a bit fuller, and the house would disappear from sight. *Probably just the way the guy likes it. Private.*

A bad feeling sank down into the pit of his stomach. Charlie didn't think Old Red wanted uninvited visitors, but there was no turning back now. Katherine took his hand once again, quietly urging him to push himself on this journey of discovery. He straightened his shoulders and they took the cobblestone path that led around the house to the side door when they caught sight of a white-haired man sitting by his outdoor fireplace.

The owner turned at the sound of their approach and inched his way up from his seat, taking hold of a carved walking stick to hobble stiffly toward them. For an instant, Charlie could have believed the hunched man had been around for the Gillette murder, he moved so slowly. Then the last rays of the dying day caught his face, glinting off his wire-framed glasses. Not so old.

With a start, Charlie bit off a curse. He'd seen that face—on the back cover of a book that he'd read and nearly burned. *Chester Gillette: Sharp-Dressed Monster. The Coward Behind the Clothes.* To say it was scathing didn't do it justice. Old Red must have written under a pen name. Charlie wanted to turn back the way they came, but it was too late. Red Foster had closed the gap between them. "Can I help you?" he asked gruffly, his twisted, arthritic hands wrapping around his cane.

Twisted. Like the man. Charlie ignored the voice in his head and offered his hand. "Mr. Foster, I'm Charlie Baxter, and this is Katherine Brown. We've been researching the Gillette-Brown murder case for a book I'm working on, trying to get to the bottom of what happened. We were told you might be able to help us."

With a bark of rough laughter, Red Foster gestured to his fireplace. "I don't know if you will consider it a help or a hindrance, but I'll tell you all I know…and you *don't* want to know. I know who you are, Baxter."

Conversation ceased as they crossed the yard to sit in Adirondack chairs flanking the fire. Red winced as he sank down in his chair, his breath going out in a hiss as his face became pinched. "Damned arthritis. I'm only sixty, but my body's twisted like a pretzel. Can't fish. Can't type. Can't even pick up a pencil anymore. Got to record my words if I have anything to say…and that well has just about dried up." He grimaced and gestured toward his cottage. "I've got some good whiskey in the house if you want to light a fire inside you. I know it's getting nippy. I've already self-medicated." Charlie and Katherine politely declined…and still, Charlie wanted to leave before too many words spilled from Foster's mouth.

Darkness settled in around them, and a hush fell over the water. Gazing off at the surface cast in silver, Red's voice dropped low. "I often picture that the night Grace died must have been like this, without a sound except the water lapping against the shore and the side of her boat. That and the sound of her screams before she went to a watery grave."

Katherine rubbed her arms, a shiver running through her that had nothing to do with the chill in the air. "We've got a pretty good impression of what that night was like ourselves."

Red stared at the flames, the shadows dancing over his face, etching the wrinkles even more deeply. He nodded and turned to meet Charlie's gaze. "I'm sure you have, especially young Charlie here. Word gets around any time someone starts digging up the skeletons in the Gillette closet. Related, aren't you, on your mother's side? Bet it really eats at you, knowing there was a cold-blooded murderer in the family. If you've come to hear something else, you've come to the wrong place."

Charlie's jaw clenched as the urge to defend his family nearly unleashed his tongue. Keeping a firm grip on his temper, he asked, "Can you give me any information that might help me with my story?"

"You're not going to like it." Red stared him down, his expression grim. There'd be no sugarcoating it.

"I don't like any of it. I don't think anyone does. What do you know that the world doesn't know already? Most say this case is like an open book. Cut-and-dried, according to George Ward, with his hundred-plus pieces of circumstantial evidence. Open and shut, right?" Charlie shrugged. His shirt felt too tight, and it was getting hard to breathe. He itched to loosen the buttons on his collar, but he didn't want to give Foster the satisfaction of knowing his words had made their way under his skin like splinters driving him to distraction.

Old Red smiled, but there was no warmth or humor in his expression or his eyes. "I have a brother's last words…in a letter that no one else was aware of. You remember Paul Gillette? Of course you do. That's how you're related. Paul took himself as far away as possible from New York after Chester was sent to fry. The whole family did, just up and abandoned him. Started a new life where no one would know they were connected to *the* notorious Chester Gillette."

He paused and let the words sink in as the fire crackled. Somewhere nearby, the mournful sound of a loon cried out. Charlie likened that loneliness to what Chester must have felt in that prison cell, completely cut off, waiting to die. *That loon can't even touch his despair. Just a drop in the bucket.* Charlie knew, firsthand, from his dream. Before they flipped the switch, he stared at a pit of sorrow so dark and so deep, there was no way out.

Foster's voice broke the silence once again. "Paul Gillette went off to A&M University in Texas. Went on to live a full life and never talked about his big brother Chester…until he was dying. Something must have nagged at him—maybe his conscience? He told his wife to read Chester's last letter. It told Paul to live a Christian life, to not let himself get tangled up in the treacherous web of a woman or he might never find his way out."

128

Charlie rose to his feet and began to pace. After a few steps, he whipped around, his hands tightening into fists. "I've heard of that letter, Mr. Foster. That doesn't prove he's guilty."

"What about his family turning their backs on him? They didn't even arrange for his burial, and they were devout Christians. Over-the-top, extreme Christians who gave up everything to lead others toward the light. What does that say about his innocence? They all walked away, Charlie. Everyone except Hazel...and she was so young, the woman was probably delusional."

"Or maybe she saw the glimmer of hope that no one else did." Charlie approached their host and stopped beside him. He was shaking with barely contained fury. "Everyone had Chester guilty from the get-go, their scapegoat. George Ward gathered a hundred pieces of evidence! Every bit of it was circumstantial! He took those letters from Chester's room in Cortland, he went after everything relentlessly—just to prove he wasn't wrong. Not to find the truth."

Foster shook his head. "You're delusional, just like your great, great-aunt, Hazel, God rest her soul. It must run in the family. There's no other explanation for Grace Brown's death except cold-hearted murder from the selfish bastard who drowned her out on that lake! He didn't see any other way to clean up his mess. Better just get rid of it...get rid of Grace!" Streaks of red marred the man's face, and his breathing was labored.

Great. Work him up, Charlie. Give him a heart attack. That will balance the scales. What was it about this case that made people rabid? He dropped down in a chair to seem less confrontational, all the fight going out of him. He was so tired of all of it. "He never admitted his guilt. Not in his final letters. Not to the prison guards. Not even in his journal. As for whatever he told the pastor the night before he died, what the hell was that supposed to mean? Anyone about to be fried in the chair would ask God in heaven and all that is holy for forgiveness of their sins. That doesn't mean he did it. What if it was a terrible accident and Chester panicked?"

"Now, wouldn't that turn this into a nice bedtime story? Fairytales aren't real, son." Red pulled himself to his feet, agonizing inch by inch to meet Charlie's eye. He stepped up close, glowering at him, fire in his eyes. "What about Gillette's composure the day he walked his final mile? You've read the papers with firsthand accounts. The man never faltered, never flinched. Wouldn't an innocent man have been pleading, begging, crying for mercy. Frantic? No, this was a cool, calculated killer."

Charlie raked a hand through his hair, shaking. The man had him quaking to the core. "He was twenty-three when it all came crashing down. Do you remember twenty-three? He was twenty-four when he died. Selfish and immature when his journey began, yes, but read his journal and you'll see. He was an old man by the time he walked to that godforsaken chair." He squeezed his eyes shut and shuddered at the memory from his nightmare. "Do you really believe he was such a monster?"

Red wouldn't back down. He would've done the prosecution proud. "If we believe for an instant that Chester didn't mean to kill her, he didn't try too hard to save Grace, did he? He tried to save his own skin and didn't tell anyone. What does that say about the man? Not only that, he barely gave her the time of day in his journal. Not the sign of a penitent man."

Charlie gritted his teeth. "I read the journal. Front to back. I went to Hamilton and held it in my hands. Maybe you have to read between the lines."

Katherine, unable to be quiet, spoke softly. "Maybe he cared too much."

The old man crossed his arms and set his jaw. He looked like a bulldog, tenaciously holding on to his bone. Red Foster wasn't going to let go of his preconceived ideas—just like everyone else. Like district attorney and future judge, George Ward. "His final entry…his last statement…his letter to his brother, telling him, *Don't let a woman make a mess of your life like I did*…his calm manner as he walked to the chair, to his death, dammit! No remorse. No regrets. He never cracked. You're climbing a mountain of guilt that is too high, Baxter."

Charlie took a step closer, his hands still in fists, but he kept his voice calm. Controlled. "Maybe Chester came to accept his fate…maybe he felt he was getting his due, that even if he didn't kill Grace, it is true he didn't save her. A life for a life, Mr. Foster. No matter what happened, don't you think he paid enough? Don't you think it's time we put Chester Gillette's soul to rest? It wasn't only Grace Brown who lost her life that night on Big Moose Lake. Chester's ended the moment she went under the water. They were both in over their heads."

His voice died out. Katherine's reassuring presence held steady at his side. Always at his side, her warmth helped him to stave off a chill, keeping him from shaking so hard his teeth would chatter. She took his arm and nodded to the historian. "We've taken enough of your time. Thank you for sharing what you did. We should go."

Charlie murmured in agreement and tucked her arm under his, turning to leave when he felt a hand on his shoulder. Red spoke gruffly. "Son, I'm sorry I was too hard on you. If it was my kin, I'd feel the same. I'd turn over every stone I could find, looking for redemption, anything that might offer an explanation. To make people understand, one way or the other. I think you need to tell your story, too. Everybody needs to read it with new eyes. Maybe finally close this book."

Charlie shook his head. "Unless I can bring them both back from the grave, I think I've hit a dead end, sir. Thank you for your time. Good night."

They walked back to the car, Charlie's feet dragging as if anchors were tying him down. He opened Katherine's door and went around to his side. Slowly, he sank into his seat and stared out over the lake. "I'm so tired. Deathly tired…I don't think I can do this anymore."

She rested her hand on his arm. "Yes, you can, but not tonight. It's late. Let's go back to Indian Lake and stay the night. Things will look different in the morning."

Charlie took a deep breath and turned the key in the ignition. They went back to a motel in town, booking a room to share. With an unspoken agreement, neither wanted to be alone with their thoughts that night. He sank down on the mattress and pulled out his phone, punching in his mother's number before he could stop himself.

"Hello?" His mother's voice nearly stopped him cold.

Charlie leaned forward and threaded his hand through his hair. "Mom? Yeah, I'm fine…well, really, I'm not. I'm awful, and I think I'm going out of my mind. No…don't try and lay any more guilt on me. I have seen and learned more than anyone ever should on this case. I'm dropping it. It will have to remain unsolved. I'm not publishing more to incriminate Chester. I'm telling you right now—there is no good news, no light at the end of the tunnel."

She pleaded with him. Begged him not to give up, to stay the course just a little longer. "Mom, if I keep at it, you're going to lose more than our family's reputation, because this case is killing me. Good night, Mom. I'll talk to you soon when I've pulled myself together."

Katherine had changed and was already in bed. She didn't say a word as he went to the bathroom to splash his face with cold water and take off his button-down shirt, along with his belt. Out of a sense of propriety, he kept his pants on and slid into bed beside her. He wanted nothing more than to lose himself in her warm, willing arms. As she shut off the light, he whispered, "Good night, Katherine. I'm sorry I dragged you into this."

She stroked his hair from his face, her voice and touch soothing. "You didn't drag me into anything. Get some sleep, Charlie. You'll catch your second wind soon."

He was restless in the night, even as she drifted off beside him. He tossed and turned. Thunder boomed and lightning crackled across the sky as ominous clouds rolled in, illuminating the room in bursts of light, shredding the darkness. It did nothing to calm his mind.

His brain was a muddle with all his research, Foster's words swirling round and round. It made him feel like he was about to be turned inside out. Too much information was crammed in his head. He wondered if this was how Adam felt when he ate from the Tree of Knowledge.

Charlie pictured Chester's journal, giving him a voice. It was the only document that shared the accused's thoughts. His sister, Hazel, kept it all those years. She was the only person who never gave up on him—the only family member who didn't turn her back on him, remaining in Auburn until her brother died. Because of Hazel, his journal was passed down and placed in the Hamilton College library thanks to his grandniece. Someone valued Chester's last words. *Why couldn't you have set the record straight? Damnation or redemption. Which was it?*

Charlie's stomach churned. Who was he kidding? This story simply would not leave him alone. There had to be a way, short of drugging or drinking himself to death. Amnesia. Maybe he could come down with amnesia. Get struck by a bolt of lightning. He shied away from that thought. *Been there, done that.* Even if it was man-made. He flipped over again. This time, he didn't even try to stop the tears running down his face. A hand, soft and gentle, rested on his side. With that touch, sleep came for him, dragging him down—but it didn't give him peace.

14

KATHERINE ROLLED OVER AND RESTED HER ARM ON CHARLIE'S SIDE. She'd heard a catch in his breathing as a tremor running through his rigid frame made her quiver. With her touch, his body went loose and he finally dropped off into sleep. As a calm settled over them, she fell into a dream of a small, simple room. It was furnished with just a chest of drawers, a table, a chair, and a small bed. The window was open. A Victrola played, "Bill Bailey, Won't You Please Come Home?" and the soft strains drifted on the air.

Wine, glistening a ruby red, sat in a bottle on the small table. Flowers, a splash of yellow, brightened the darkness. She was dancing with a tall, dark-haired man; he smelled heavenly, his cologne making her dizzy with every turn around the room. This man. He had her from the start, the first time she saw that smile and the way his eyes warmed when he looked at her. She rested her head on his chest. The music of his heart, thumping steadily, hummed in her ear. In her soul. His arms were strong enough to ease all her fears. "Kid…Gracie…it will be all right. I know you're scared, but I'll make it right."

Even in a dream, the words rang true. "As long as I'm with you, Chester."

Katherine awoke with the first rays of sun tiptoeing into their room. Charlie was turned toward her, one of her curls wrapped around his finger. He gave her a tired smile. The lines beside his eyes and around his mouth were etched more deeply. Clearly, his night had not gone well. She leaned forward to kiss him. His eyes drifted closed as he let out a soft sigh.

"Let's go to Big Moose today. It will be all right, Charlie. I promise. It will be all right." Chester's words and the peace that came with them echoed back to her. Seeing the shadows in Charlie's eyes, her tongue loosened, recounting every scrap of the dream she could remember, even though she wanted to hold that treasure close to her heart. Charlie needed that strength more than she did.

By the time the words ran dry, there was a hint of brightness in his gaze. "I don't know if I believe it, Katherine, but I'll take anything I can get right now. Foster said I believed in fairytales last night. No matter what we learn about this case, there is no shining knight on a white horse, no magic fairy to break the spell. Grace and Chester are long gone. Nothing can bring either of them back."

Katherine rested her forehead against his. "You can give them peace, Charlie. If anyone can, it's you—because you won't give up. You can give us peace."

THE RIDE WAS NEARLY AN HOUR. Katherine tried to stay awake, but the late nights and emotional drain of the past few days had caught up to her. As the tides of sleep pulled her under, the undertow of dreams sucked her down—deep. Into the nightmare from her first night, the night she'd met Charlie. The night their paths intersected, and they began traveling the same road. This time, a paddle smacked Grace upside the head before she went overboard.

Not a tennis racket.

Horrified by the twist her mind had taken, Katherine fought it, even in her dream, until a soft voice whispered in her mind. *It didn't happen like that. Chester didn't strike me…he would never lay a hand on me to harm me…never hurt me in that way.*

Katherine's eyes snapped open and she jerked up in her seat, coming up fast from a slouch against the window. Staring at the glass, she saw the face of a woman with dark hair pulled up on the top of her head, her white dress fluttering in the breeze. Her sorrowful eyes rested on Charlie with such compassion it would make a person weep. *Charlie isn't the only one who's cracking under the strain.*

"Hey, you okay?" A hand pressed hers, snagging her attention. Charlie watched her closely, clearly troubled. When she glanced back at the window, the image was gone. Katherine sagged in relief.

"I'm fine, just fine. I thought I saw something…something on the side of the road. Nothing is there." She tucked a strand of hair behind her ear and gave him what she hoped was a smile of reassurance. Her face turned to the window once again, but her mind was caught in that dream.

That first time, that night she awoke screaming in terror, only the ending had played out. Katherine never saw how Grace managed to end up going overboard. She'd hoped after that night of sleepwalking and a dousing in the pond, this particular nightmare would not make a comeback.

If she closed her eyes, Katherine could almost feel the impact of that oar upside her head. Her heart began to hammer, her mouth going dry. Her hands curled into fists as she focused on the passing scenery and prayed they'd get there soon. She just wanted it to be over, to discover the truth. If that was even possible.

You know exactly what happened. Grace has shown you.

The ramifications of that realization remained to be seen. Somehow, Katherine and Charlie were both connected to that distant day, entangled in a web they could not escape. Taking a deep breath, her eyes slid his way. His forehead was creased with worry, his hands tight on the wheel. Today marked the end of the road, the final journey, and it couldn't be easy on him. She reached out and stroked his hair, hoping to ease him…and a heart worn raw. Letting her breath out, one she'd been holding for too long, she gave him a genuine smile. He returned the favor.

HOW IRONIC. THE GLENMORE HOTEL WAS STILL OPEN FOR BUSINESS. The place where Chester and Grace stayed on their last night together, overlooking the lake where they both lost their lives. Chester's death just took a little longer. With grim determination, Charlie paid for their room and took Katherine with him to Duffy's, the hotel restaurant. The setting was warm and inviting, with the low hum of conversation rolling over him and a beautiful woman across the table. Why did it feel like he was about to face a firing squad?

"Charlie, you really ought to eat something. You've hardly touched anything in days." Katherine took a sip of her tea and reached across the table to link her hand in his. He held on like a man about to drown.

"I'm sorry. I'm just not hungry." For her sake, he forced himself to sit up and eat the bowl of soup before him. As for his sandwich, he swallowed a few bites and he was done. He wondered…did Chester eat well when they gave him his final breakfast? That thought made his stomach twist, and he excused himself to the bathroom. He stood at the sink and fought to keep his lunch down, dousing his face in cold water, pressing a wet paper towel to his neck.

Two men walked in and went to the urinals. They didn't pay Charlie any mind. "Can you believe Irene is dragging us out there after dark tonight? Ever since she saw that episode of *Unsolved Mysteries*, she's fallen for it hook, line, and sinker. A ghost sighting! I'd rather be watching the Yanks."

Charlie's stomach pitched unpleasantly, and he made for the isolation of a stall. He clamped his hand over his mouth and swallowed hard. A cold sweat sprang up, but he managed to keep down what little he'd eaten. He didn't step out until the men left, and then he took a deep breath. Katherine was waiting for him. With a determined set to his shoulders, he headed back out into the dining room.

Katherine started to rise as soon as he approached, but he waved her down. "Are you all right? You were gone quite a while."

"I'm fine." He took a sip of his coffee but found it to be bitter. "I see you're done. Why don't we take a walk, try and get something good out of this day? I don't think it will be showtime until tonight, if anything is going to happen at all. I have my serious doubts." At her agreement, he peeled out several bills and laid them on the table. He offered Katherine his hand and led her out without looking back. Charlie didn't want to hear any more about Grace Brown ghost hunters. *Isn't that what you are?* the cynical voice in his head questioned him. He ignored it.

The day passed pleasantly enough—walking through the quaint town, by the shore of the lake, on a nature trail. Perching on a rock and staring out over the water. Putting off the inevitability of nightfall, but the sunset came anyway. He couldn't stop time. Charlie had a feeling he couldn't change anything about what happened with Chester and Grace, either, including setting the record straight.

A feeling of utter hopelessness washed over him, nearly flattening him as they turned into their bedroom for the night. He tried to hide it from Katherine, taking to the balcony as the moon became a brilliant beacon in the darkness. He closed his eyes tightly as the date drove its way home. July 11th. The anniversary of Grace Mae Brown's death over 110 years ago. Charlie hadn't even planned to be here. Perhaps, like Chester, this was his part to play, and it was impossible to walk away.

Grace! Tell Grace! The voice, usually a soft whisper on the edge of consciousness, practically shouted in his ear. Charlie gripped the railing and closed his eyes. *Please, Chester. Can't you leave me alone? I've done all I can. I can't bring her back. Let me be!*

Katherine laid a hand on his back, making him jump. With a gasp, his head snapped up and he scanned the lake below. Nothing. A glimpse out of the corner of his eye proved that Chester did not stand beside him. *Maybe he never did and you're out of your mind.*

"Charlie, it's getting late. Why don't you come to bed?" She moved in front of him and looped her arms around his neck, her gaze steady, calming the storm. "You've done enough."

He rested his head on hers. "Don't you see, Katherine? It wasn't enough. Not nearly enough." Weary beyond words, he didn't fight her as she led him to the bed, helped him to shed his clothes, and held out his pajama bottoms. "Are you sure you want to stay here tonight, of all nights?"

She slid under the covers beside him and stared into his eyes, a small smile creeping up. "I know this is going to sound strange, but being here of all places, with you by my side, I've felt the calmest I have in a long time—like I'm meant to be here, now, at peace. I think we both are."

He bowed his head. It felt like a great weight was wrapped around his neck, ready to pull him under. "I just want it to be over, finally. No more visions, nightmares, questions, doubts. I want my life back. I want to spend it with you." Charlie's hand hovered tentatively before settling on her cheek. "Thank you for being so patient with me today, Katherine. I'll make it up to you."

"Make it up to me by sleeping now." With that, she ducked in to brush his lips lightly with a kiss, her mouth turned up in a smile. It was the last thing he saw before sleep took him.

"KATHERINE?" CHARLIE SAT UP WITH ONE MIGHTY THRUST, breaking free from the shreds of dreams that continued to cling to his mind. Something wasn't right. She wasn't lying next to him.

He slid his feet over the side of the bed and shot up, darting out to the balcony first. No sign there. He came back inside and checked the bathroom, ducked his head outside, even considered going down to the lobby. All the while, a nagging voice in his head—one that sounded like Chester—told him to go back outside.

Dreading what he might find, he gazed out over the water only to see a ghostly boat far out in the middle of the lake. If he squinted, it was possible to see through it to the other side. It wasn't the boat that sent ice running through his veins and nearly stopped his heart. It was the retreating figure of a woman, walking toward the lake, her feet carrying her closer to that boat with every step. *Katherine!* "Chester, why are you doing *this*? Haven't you done enough?"

Nobody answered him. Charlie didn't even have time to put on his shoes. He scrambled down the outdoor set of stairs, vaulting over the last few. His bare feet pounded across the sand as Katherine continued to wade into the water, deeper with every step, like the night on the pond. But tonight, Charlie feared she might follow Grace to a terrible ending.

"Katherine! Stop! Stop right now! *Wake up!*" he shouted as his feet hit the water, ready to dive in and get to her.

In that instant, she turned around, her eyes wide with shock and fright. Unable to register where she was or what was happening, her face crumpled. Charlie reached her, and she fell into his arms. "Charlie! Oh, Charlie! I don't know what happened."

He wrapped an arm around her, and slowly, they made their way out of the lake. Both refused to turn around and acknowledge the boat on the water. If those events were going to play out again, there would be two fewer witnesses.

As soon as their feet hit the shore, Charlie threaded his fingers through Katherine's hair. "You look at me, Katherine. Look at *me* right now. I am real, I'm here, and I'm yours. Nothing else matters." His head tilted and his lips touched down on hers.

A small cry escaped her. "And I'm yours, Charlie!" Her fingers dug into the thin fabric of his T-shirt and she gave herself to another kiss.

A warm breeze drifted over them with the scent of honeysuckle. Music floated on the air around them. They were not alone. Katherine stepped back first, and her breath came out in a rush. "Look," she whispered, her hand rising to cover her mouth.

Charlie lifted his head to see two figures walking toward each other in the moonlight. A man with dark hair in a dark suit. A woman in white with her hair pinned up on top of her head. He held out his hand and she accepted, stepping into the wall of his chest.

In Charlie's mind, he could hear a deep voice. Chester's voice. Katherine jerked beside him. She heard it, too. *I didn't mean it, Gracie. Dear God, I didn't mean for you to fall out of the boat. I tried to save you, but I was too late and I didn't know what to do. I love you, Gracie. Only you! Walking away from you, a marriage, our baby, was the biggest mistake I could have made, and I paid for it with my life. If I could go back, I would've jumped out of that boat and given myself to spare you.*

She gazed up at him, and her hand rested on his cheek. *I know, Chester. I loved you from the start and I never stopped. All these years, I've been searching for you.*

Silver tracks ran down Chester's face, mingling with Grace's tears as his hands came up to cup her cheeks. He kissed her long and slow, a kiss meant to bind the wounds that had been gaping between them, to right the wrongs. A kiss that could last for eternity. The music swelled and the breeze pulled at Charlie and Katherine as the reunited couple began to dance. Slowly, wrapped in each other's arms, they became a white, glowing light, so bright that Charlie and Katherine had to close their eyes. When they looked again, the beach was empty. No ghostly boat floated on Big Moose Lake. Only the quiet sigh of the wind in the trees and the lapping of the water as it kissed the shore kept them company.

Charlie whispered, as if afraid to break the spell. "I'm going to write their story, but no one will believe it."

Katherine squeezed his hand. "You do… and so do I. Nothing else matters."

He had no idea how much time went by until Katherine's shivering shook Charlie from his thoughts. "Let's go back to bed. You're freezing." Slowly, they walked back to their room and helped each other to change, both chilled to the point of trembling.

Charlie pulled up the covers and held Katherine close in an attempt to warm her. She snuggled against his chest and whispered, "I keep seeing them, Grace and Chester, and the love in their eyes, the smiles on their faces."

Charlie stroked her hair. "The only thing I see is you, Katherine. After all this, I can't live without you. Will you stay with me?"

Her tears spilled over and wet the pillow as she nodded. "Do you think I've finally found the right guy and the place I belong?"

He nodded and rubbed his thumb on her cheek. "When I'm with you, I'm where I belong. I come home."

She reached out with trembling fingers and placed his hand on her heart. "Can you hear it? The door is open. Come in and stay awhile. Scratch that. Stay forever."

As they drifted off in each other's arms, music wafted into their room. "Won't you come home, Bill Bailey?" it played. Charlie couldn't help but smile as the crack in his heart was finally mended. Laughter, high and bright, followed by a deep rumble, echoed off the walls. Chester and Grace had a homecoming as well. Charlie closed his eyes and sighed softly.

You got your happy ending, Ma.

Afterword

On July 11, 1906, a young woman by the name of Grace Mae Brown was discovered floating, dead, in Big Moose Lake in the Adirondacks of upstate New York. Tragedy struck on the day following what was supposed to be a pleasant boating excursion on a supposed wedding or honeymoon trip. Foul play was suspected, and her traveling companion, Chester Gillette, was apprehended soon after in the Arrowhead Hotel, not far away in Inlet.

The scandalous turn of events led to the trial of the century, capturing the imagination and fascination of the nation. By December of 1906, Gillette was found guilty and sentenced to death. He died in the electric chair in March of 1908. Several books, both fictional and non-fictional, have been inspired by this tale: Theodore Dreiser's *An American Tragedy*, Craig Brandon's *Murder in the Adirondacks*, Joseph Brownell's *An Adirondack Tragedy*, Jennifer Donnelly's *A Northern Light*, and the film *A Place in the Sun*. The case has continued to breed curiosity as people raise questions and wonder what really happened out there on the water. If only the dead could talk.

Ward's Pond and the prosecutor's home are only thirty minutes away from my home in Johnstown, not too far from where the notorious events took place. The references made concerning Grace and Gillette's story actually did come from the *New York Times* back in 1905 and 1906. Chester's parting words from his journal excerpt, a public domain, are truly his own.

I've sat in the dining room sipping tea, stared up at Judge Ward's stern portrait, stood on his porch. I've looked out at his pond as the geese settled in. As I talked about writing with the innkeeper, Elaina, and held a book signing, I couldn't help but be captivated by a copy of *Murder in the Adirondacks* sitting on the shelf, especially the pictures of Chester...so dashing and handsome, and the young Grace, so sweet and innocent. It's hard to believe that only a little over a hundred years ago, their story would make national headlines, and now it continues to live on today.

Soon after, I had to watch *A Place in the Sun*. Montgomery Clift's desperation and Shelly Winters' hopelessness drew me in deeper. I felt as if I'd stirred up ghosts by visiting Ward's Pond. If you get a chance to drop in one day, especially as the sun is touching down, the willow trees reflected in the pond and the stillness will wrap itself around you. Surrender, and you might walk with ghosts of the past yourself at Ward's Pond as a true American tragedy makes you wonder.

What really did happen that fateful day? Did Chester kill Grace? Did she commit suicide, as he insisted during the trial? Or was it an accident that will never allow their ghosts to rest? This tragic secret is buried with Chester Gillette and Grace Brown. It's up to you to decide what really happened on that eerie summer night over one hundred years ago when Grace and Chester went out on Big Moose Lake...but only Chester came back.

Heidi Sprouse lives in upstate NY in historic Johnstown. She attended college at St. Rose in Albany, knowing all along her two loves were teaching and English. It took four years before she landed the teaching job of her dreams, but over twenty years later she is still nurturing little ones in re-K. She loves the privilege of watching brand-new little humans as they discover and begin to shape their own worlds.

Knowing what she wants and going after it in relentless pursuit is Sprouse's gift. Deciding to become an author can be downright unnerving, but Sprouse bit into the challenge, took off, and never looked back. Her perseverance proves success is not a matter of luck. It's a matter of finding what speaks to your heart and committing to do that thing until it makes a difference.

When she isn't busy teaching or with her husband Jim, her son Patrick, and her canine kids Chuck and Dale, she's cooking up her next novel. She dabbles in sweet romances, historical fiction, and suspense thrillers, depending on what pleases her reader's eye at any given moment. Sprouse is always in search of the extraordinary in the ordinary, writing about strong men with old-fashioned values and the women who pick them up when they fall. She'll tell anyone it's never too late to chase after your dreams, no dream is too small or insignificant, and any mountain can be moved with a proposal and a good plan.

Her past works include: *All the Little Things, Lightning Can Strike Twice, Aging Gracefully, Sunny Side Up, Against the Grain, Hope's Rise From Ashes, When You Wish Upon a Christmas Tree, Adirondack Sundown, The Edge of Forgiveness on Blue Mountain, Sunrise Over Indian Lake, Deserted on Lake Desolation, One Last Adirondack Summer, Whispers of Liberty, Liberty's Promise, Liberty's Legacy, Rosie and her Ragamuffin Sam, and Mouse.* Stay tuned for more to come!